Marco Polo for Kids

HIS MARVELOUS JOURNEY TO CHINA ✕ 21 ACTIVITIES

Marco Polo for Kids

JANIS HERBERT

CHICAGO
REVIEW
PRESS

Library of Congress Cataloging-in-Publication Data

Herbert, Janis, 1956–
    Marco Polo for kids: his marvelous journey to China: 21
activities / Janis Herbert.
        p. cm.
    Includes bibliographical references and index.
    ISBN 1-55652-377-7
    1. Polo, Marco, 1254–1323?–Journeys–China–Juvenile
literature. 2. China–Description and travel–Juvenile literature. 3. China–History–Yuan Dynasty, 1260–1368–Juvenile
literature. [1. Polo, Marco, 1254–1323?–Journeys. 2. Voyages
and travels. 3. Asia–Description and travel.] I. Title: His
marvelous journey to China: 21 activities. II. Title.
    G370.P9 H38 2001
    915.04'20–dc21   2001017474

Cover and interior design: Joan Sommers Design, Chicago

The author and the publisher disclaim all liability for use of information contained in this book.

The author has made every effort to secure permissions for all material quoted in this book. If any acknowledgment has inadvertently been omitted, please contact the publisher.

First edition
Published by Chicago Review Press, Incorporated
814 North Franklin Street
Chicago, Illinois 60610
ISBN 978-1-55652-377-9

Printed in China by C & C Offset Company, Ltd.
5 4 3 2

Front cover: (upper left) The Great Wall of China, courtesy of Northwest Archives; (bottom left) The Polos leaving Venice, courtesy of Northwest Archives; (middle)
Medieval Tartar huts and wagons, courtesy of Northwest
Archives; (middle, bottom) Marco Polo lands at Ormuz,
courtesy of Northwest Archives.

Back cover: (upper right) Caravan on the great highway
of Central Asia, courtesy of Northwest Archives; (upper
left) Frontispiece from Polo's *Voyages*, published in
Nuremberg, 1477, courtesy of Northwest Archives.

To Gregory, Johnny, Kate, and Sophie Pearl, with love

Contents

Acknowledgments

This book was created with the generous assistance of Wafa Barakat, Marianne Coogan, Sara Dickinson, Olivia Lenny Hill, Debbie Lenny, Ruth and Don Ross, and Sarah Shaar. They have my warmest thanks for sharing their talent and expertise and for offering their encouragement. Thanks once again to designer Joan Sommers and to all of the people at Chicago Review Press. Special thanks are due to Cynthia Sherry for her enthusiasm and devotion to this project. Thanks, again and always, to Jeff for his unwavering support.

Note to Readers

Many of the names and borders of countries have changed since Marco Polo made his famous journey. In this book, you will see the names of countries like Turkey, Sri Lanka, and Afghanistan, but Marco might have called them by other names. The glossary on page 116 will explain unfamiliar terms and places, and in the biographies section beginning on page 119, you will find additional information about historical figures who are mentioned throughout the story. For those interested in further information on topics related to Marco Polo's journey, the resource section beginning on page 121 lists Web sites to explore, and the bibliography on page 123 suggests some useful books.

Time Line

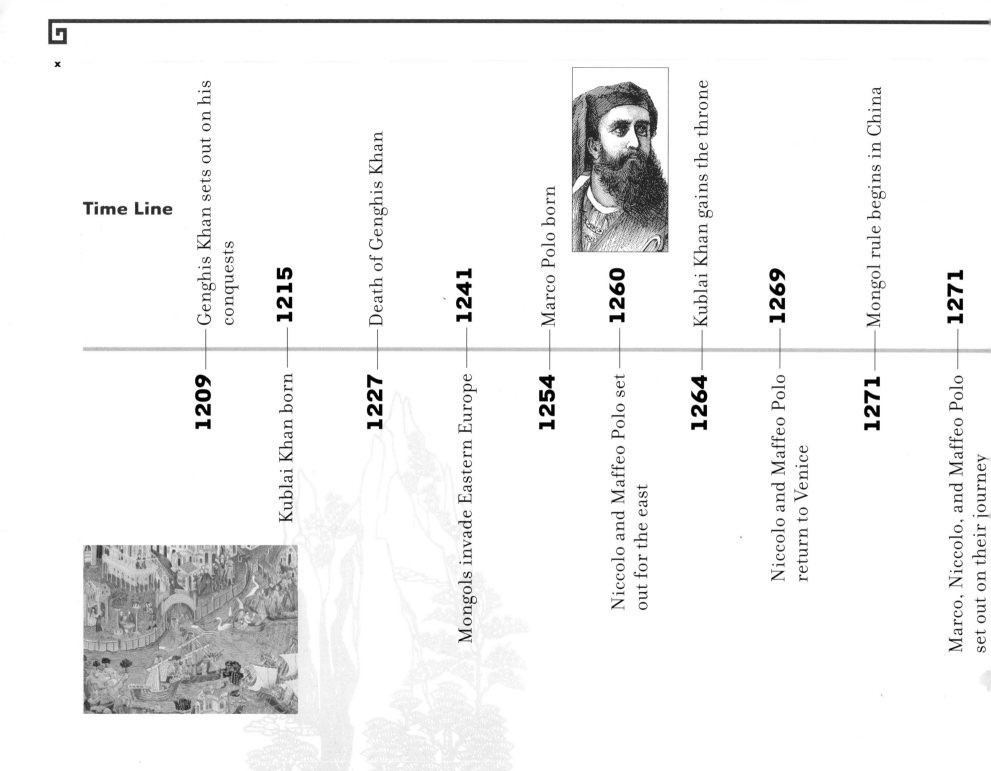

1209 — Genghis Khan sets out on his conquests

1215 — Kublai Khan born

1227 — Death of Genghis Khan

1241 — Mongols invade Eastern Europe

1254 — Marco Polo born

1260 — Niccolo and Maffeo Polo set out for the east

1264 — Kublai Khan gains the throne

1269 — Niccolo and Maffeo Polo return to Venice

1271 — Mongol rule begins in China

1271 — Marco, Niccolo, and Maffeo Polo set out on their journey

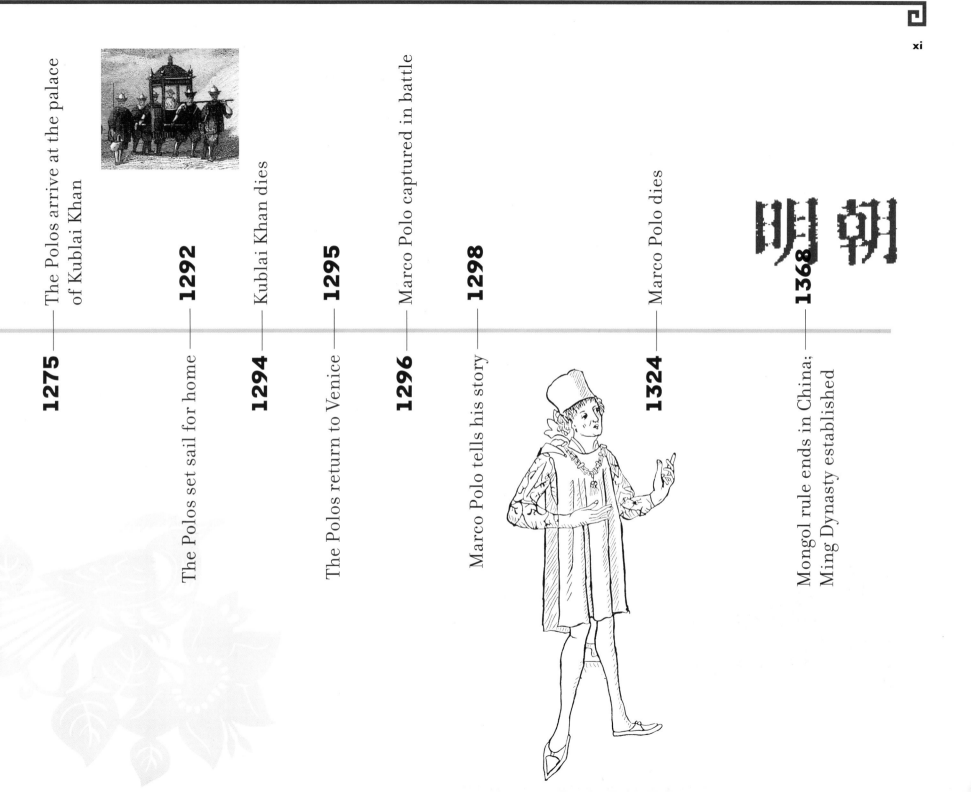

1275 — The Polos arrive at the palace of Kublai Khan

1292 — The Polos set sail for home

1294 — Kublai Khan dies

1295 — The Polos return to Venice

1296 — Marco Polo captured in battle

1298 — Marco Polo tells his story

1324 — Marco Polo dies

1368 — Mongol rule ends in China; Ming Dynasty established

明朝

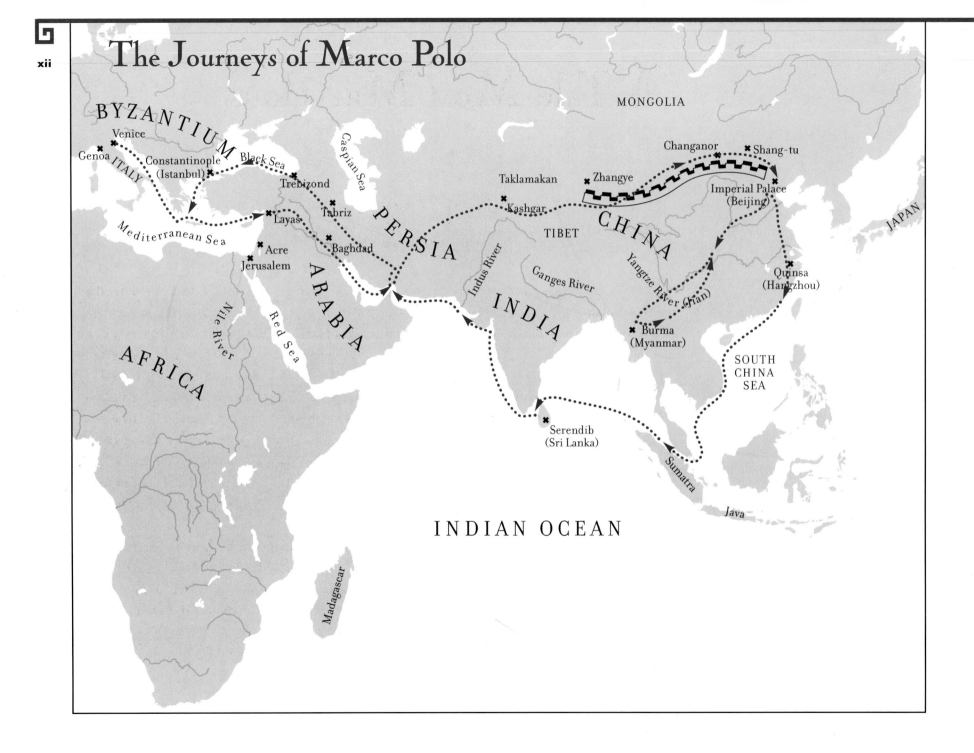

The Journeys of Marco Polo

BYZANTIUM

MONGOLIA

Venice

Genoa ITALY

Constantinople (Istanbul)

Black Sea

Trebizond

Caspian Sea

Changanor

Shang-tu

Zhangye

Taklamakan

Imperial Palace (Beijing)

Layas

Tabriz

PERSIA

Kashgar

CHINA

JAPAN

Mediterranean Sea

Baghdad

TIBET

Acre

Jerusalem

ARABIA

Indus River

INDIA

Ganges River

Yangtze River (Jian)

Quinsa (Hangzhou)

Nile River

Red Sea

AFRICA

Burma (Myanmar)

SOUTH CHINA SEA

Serendib (Sri Lanka)

Sumatra

Java

Madagascar

INDIAN OCEAN

A Tale Most Marvelous

Preface

"Tell me, Marco," Rustichello begged, "another story of your journey!"

"What would you hear next?" Marco Polo asked his fellow prisoner. The days were long in prison, and telling the story of his travels helped them to pass a little faster. "Should I tell you about the great Khan's pet leopards and the magicians at his court? Or of the conquests of his ancestor, Genghis Khan? Would you like to hear about the Old Man of the Mountains or of the desert which takes a year to cross?"

"Why don't you start at the beginning this time," said Rustichello. "I will write it all down, and make a book of your tale. Someday this book will be read the world over, and all shall know of the wonders you have seen." Marco smiled. They would never believe it, he thought.

For three years, Marco had been a prisoner of the Italian city of Genoa, since his ship had been captured in a battle between that city and his home, Venice. Before that, he had only been home for a year. From the time he was 15 years old until he was a man of 39, Marco had traveled to places no European had ever seen before.

With his father and uncle, he had sailed from Venice to the Holy Land. From there they had sailed to a trading port on the eastern Mediterranean Sea. He had traveled by caravan through vast deserts and over steep mountain ranges, stopping in exotic cities and humble villages, until he came at last to the palace of Kublai Khan in far-off China. For many years, Marco had been a favorite of the Khan's and had traveled as his emissary in the far eastern lands. Finally, he had come home, accompanying a Mongol princess in a fleet of Chinese ships.

He would tell the story of his journey— let them believe him or not! He had seen an ancient land and learned much about its people. He would share his adventures, his millions of stories.

"Speak slowly," said Rustichello. "I want to get it all down."

M arco Polo had been waiting for this day forever! His father, Niccolo, and his Uncle Maffeo had finally returned from a journey many years long. The boy had been only six when his father and uncle had left their home in Venice. Now Marco was 15! In those nine years, he had grown nearly to manhood. He had studied hard, so he could help his father with his business. When he was not studying, he spent his days wandering around Venice's busy wharves, where traders

brought ships loaded with silks and spices, dyes, salt, and wool. Marco's mother had died during his childhood, making him doubly glad for his father's safe return. Now he listened to his father and uncle tell the story of their journey, a story that made Marco thrill with excitement.

Niccolo and Maffeo were successful merchants of luxury goods in the western world's center of trade, Venice. The aim of their long journey had been to establish ties of trade with the new rulers of the lands east of the Mediterranean Sea. The people of Europe were hungry for such exotic goods such as the silks

and spices that trickled to their ports from distant lands to the east. The two Polo brothers, with trunks full of jewels to trade, had sailed to the Black Sea to visit the court of a wealthy ruler. Trading was good, and they stayed for a year. When they wished to return to Venice, however, they found that war raged across their route. Cut off from home, they decided to continue their journey in another direction.

They found themselves in strange lands among nomadic (wandering) people who herded livestock and lived in wide tents. After a long and dangerous desert crossing, they came

The Polos leave Venice

1

to a magnificent city, Bukhara. Here they made their home for three years. One day, they met an ambassador on his way to visit the supreme ruler of the Mongol Empire. The ambassador persuaded the brothers to join him on his journey to the palace of Kublai Khan, the man who ruled the largest empire in the world.

It took a year for the Polo brothers to reach their destination. Their journey took them through many countries, over high mountain ranges, and across forbidding deserts. Finally, they reached the court of Kublai Khan, where they received a warm welcome. The Khan had never met anyone from their land and was very curious about their country and customs. He asked many questions about their form of government, their religion, and their leaders. When they told him about the Pope, who was the head of their church, Kublai Khan questioned them at length. In all of his vast empire, he had subjects of many religions, but he had never before met any Christians. They told him about their beliefs and explained their religion. The Khan, who was very curious about religions, asked them to take the Pope a message. He asked that the Pope send 100 of the west's wisest men to his court, men who were masters of the "seven arts" (grammar, rhetoric, logic, arithmetic, music, geometry, and astronomy). He asked the brothers to return with the wise

Wedded to the Sea

The Italian city of Venice is known for its canals and bridges. Because of its location on the Adriatic Sea, it was also once the center for trade between the countries of the east and of the west. Its merchants grew rich on the goods that came to Venice on ships from countries such as India and Persia. Venetians still celebrate their good fortune once a year with a marriage ceremony between their city and the sea. A golden wedding ring is thrown into the water while citizens watch from decorated gondolas and ships.

Say It in Turkish

You might already speak Turkish! If you have had meat, onions, and peppers on skewers, you might have called it shish kebob—a Turkish word. Some people say "It's kismet" (fate) when something happens that seems like it was "meant to be." Here are some other Turkish words you can use:

Hello: Merhaba
(mehr-hah-bah)

Good-bye: Allaha ismar-ladik (ah-lah is-mahr-lah-dihk)

Please: Lutfen (lut-fehn)

Thank you: Tesekkur eder-im (tesh-eh-keur eh-deh-reem)

Yes: Evet (eh-veht)

No: Hayir (hah-yihr)

men and to bring him a vial of oil from a lamp in the Church of the Holy Sepulchre (the tomb of Christ in Jerusalem).

When the Polos were ready to return to their homeland, the Khan gave them a long tablet of gold marked with a special inscription. With this tablet, the brothers could obtain lodging, horses, and provisions in all of the towns along their route. While this made things a little easier, it still took them three years to get home! Snow, storms, and flooded rivers slowed their journey. Now, finally, they were home again. Marco marveled at the tales they told of distant lands and the great kingdom of Kublai Khan. Would he ever see such sights?

The Polos planned to keep their word to the Khan, but by the time they returned to Venice, the Pope had died. They had to wait a long time before a successor was named. Finally a new pope was in place, and he granted them an audience in the holy city of Acre (in Palestine). The Polos boarded a ship and set sail for the meeting place.

The Pope appointed only two friars to accompany the brothers to the Khan's palace—far short of the 100 wise men the Khan had requested. He gave letters to these friars to deliver to Kublai Khan and gave them expensive gifts of crystal to present to the ruler. He permitted the Polo brothers to take oil from the lamp burning over the sacred tomb. The Polos were now ready to return to the Khan's palace. In 1271, they set out on another long journey. This time, young Marco joined them.

Their ship took them across the Mediterranean Sea to the busy trading port of Layas. As they made preparations for a long overland journey, they heard troubling news. The Sultan of Egypt was leading a great army against his neighbors—bloodshed and destruction lay across the Polos' path! When the friars heard this news, they gave the Pope's letters and gifts to the Polos and went straight back to their monastery. They wanted no part of this dangerous expedition! The Polos, however, felt honor-bound to return to the Khan, with or without the friars. They joined a caravan (an armed group of traders traveling together for safety) and set out on horseback.

Turkey

War was nothing new in the country the Polos were about to enter. Persians, Greeks, European Crusaders, Turks, and Mongols had all fought over it. They all wanted to rule the land (present-day Turkey) that straddles the continents of Asia and Europe.

People had lived here as far back as 7000 B.C. It was the home of one of the world's most

ACTIVITY

Make a Mythical Map

The Polos were leaving for lands that many people thought were inhabited by demons and monsters! Maps from medieval Europe showed the known world (parts of Africa, Asia, and Europe centered around the Mediterranean Sea) surrounded by mythical lands. Early travelers claimed they had visited countries where people hopped along on only one foot, or had ears as large as their bodies, which they used as blankets at night! They told of talking serpents, unicorns, and griffins. There were reports of Amazons (fierce female warriors), dog-headed men, and the realm of Prester John (a legendary kingdom where rivers flowed with gold, and the Fountain of Youth made those who drank from its waters young again). Hideous monsters were said to guard mountain passes and narrow straits. "Here be dragons," the mapmakers wrote in warning along the margins of their maps. Try making your own mythical map.

What you need

Scissors

Brown paper grocery bag

Markers or paints and brushes

Damp tea bag

8-inch-long piece of red ribbon

Cut the bag into a large, flat surface for your map. Draw continents and oceans, countries and rivers. Make up bizarre people and animals to inhabit this world—fire-breathing serpents that guard mountain passes, or dog-headed people who bark at passing ships! Fill your map with pictures and warnings. When you're done drawing and painting, scrunch the map up in your hands, then flatten it out again to give it an antique look. To make it look even more like an ancient map on parchment, rip away little pieces at the edges and smudge it in places by pressing a damp tea bag against the paper to stain it. Let it dry, then roll it up and tie it with the red ribbon.

ancient civilizations, the Hittites. The land was ruled for centuries by the Persians until they were driven out by Alexander the Great, a young Greek general who built an empire that reached from Greece to Egypt and India.

In the fourth century, Emperor Constantine took control of the Roman Empire and moved its capital here, to a great city that took his name—Constantinople, now known as Istanbul. Six hundred years later, this Eastern Roman Empire fell under the arrows of a nomadic Turkish tribe. These fierce warriors from Asia threatened all of Europe. The Christian pope urged the knights and nobles of Europe to destroy them. (This was the beginning of the wars called the Crusades.) Later, another Turkish tribe, the Ottomans, would invade the land. They crowned their sultan the "Emperor of Mighty Emperors, Terror of All the World" and created an empire that lasted for hundreds of years.

In Marco Polo's time, the country had recently been invaded by a group of warriors from Asia called the Mongols. With all this fighting going on, it was no wonder the two friars didn't want to go any farther. In spite of war and danger, the caravan moved on. Each mile brought new marvels. Wide-eyed Marco wrote notes about their travels and experiences. At first, they found themselves in rough plateau

Caravan on the great highway of central Asia

Weave a Wall Hanging

Weaving is one of the most ancient arts in the world. Marco saw people weaving beautiful carpets on their looms. In this activity, you can weave an artwork for your wall. Here are two words you should know—"warp" means the threads that run the long way (up and down); "woof" means the threads that you weave back and forth (sideways).

Adult supervision required

What you need

Pencil

Ruler

Large, sturdy cardboard box (order a pizza
   and use the box)

60 nails, any size

Skein of yarn or ball of string

Scissors

Assortment of colored yarn, raffia, and ¼-inch-
   wide strips of cloth—all in your favorite colors

Assortment of beads, feathers, and buttons
   (optional)

Plain piece of cloth, 15 inches by 8 inches

Needle and thread or sewing machine

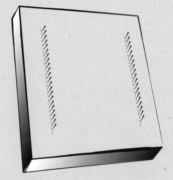

1 To make the loom, draw two parallel lines, 15 inches long and 8 inches apart, on the outside of the box. Make a mark every ½ inch along each line. Push nails through at these marks, leaving them sticking out about ¼ inch above the surface of the box.

2 Tie a piece of yarn or string to the nail on the top left (as shown in the illustration). Pull it across the box to the opposite nail and pull it around the head of that nail. Pull it back up and circle around the nail to the right of the first one. Continue doing this until you reach the last nail. Tie the yarn or string in a knot around this nail and cut off the leftover string. These strings now form the warp on your loom.

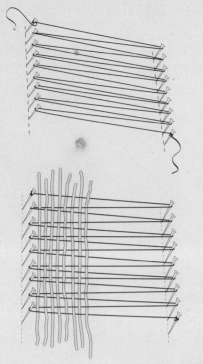

3 Start weaving from the bottom up by threading a new piece of yarn or string over and under the warp threads. Go over one thread, then under the next, over the next, and so on. Turn around when you reach the end and this time do the opposite of what you did on the way across. Go under, then over, then under. Don't pull too tight. As you weave, push the woof thread down close against the thread below it so there aren't any big gaps.

4 Add different colors and textures by cutting your yarn or string and tying onto the end a different color of yarn, raffia, or strip of cloth. Weave in beads, feathers, or buttons if you want. Change colors and textures and fabrics as you go along. If you like, you can change the pattern of the weave—for example, skip two warps and go under the next one, or weave halfway across, then backtrack.

5 When you reach the end, carefully remove the nails from the box. Place the woven piece on top of the plain cloth and sew it all the way around the edges. Hang your woven art work on your wall.

country where shepherds herded their livestock over grassy plains, wore clothes made of skins, and lived in felt tents. Then they passed through bustling cities where craftspeople and traders jostled each other in noisy bazaars (marketplaces). The people here wove the finest carpets in the world, in designs of exquisite color and beauty. All day, they sat cross-legged in front of their looms, twisting and weaving with nimble fingers. A carpet took months to make.

Persian carpet

The Polos' route took them over twisting mountain roads with long views of steep, rocky ridges. The country "abounded in castles and cities," wrote Marco. Then it grew wilder, the mountains rose higher, and their path became more treacherous. Finally the land opened up before them and they saw an amazing sight—the high peak of Mount Ararat. Shepherds grazed their horses and sheep on the mountain's slopes. Others brought casks to the mountain to collect oil from a gushing spring. Marco found it astounding that they used this oil, not to eat, but to burn in lamps—who had ever heard of such a thing? Mount Ararat, Marco wrote, was "the Mountain of the Ark, on which it is said Noah's ark came to rest."

Marco made notes about the geography of the countries they passed through, their forms of government, and the customs of their people. He paid special attention to things that would be of interest to his trading family, such as the types of goods produced. Local legends and stories made a great impression on him. In one country, he noted, the "kings were born with the mark of an eagle on the right shoulder." In another, people wove "material known as mosulin from silk and gold thread." Over and over again he wrote that the countries were under the rule of the "Tartars"— the nomadic Mongolian tribes that had lately come to power.

Noah's Ark and the Great Flood

The story of Noah, who built a ship large enough to hold two of each animal to save them from a great flood, is similar to stories told by people throughout the world. In China, it is Sago-king Yu who saved his country from a great flood. In India, it is said that Manu built a boat and, guided by a sacred fish, landed safely on a mountaintop. Hawaiian, African, and Native American peoples tell similar tales.

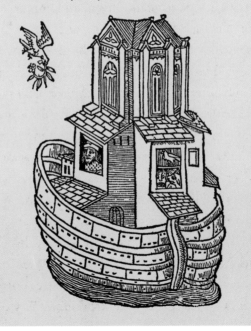

Marco was traveling through a vast empire—the Mongol Empire.

The Mongol Empire

Less than 100 years before Marco Polo started his journey, a boy named Temujin lived on the distant Mongolian steppes (plains). Temujin had been born with a blood clot in the palm of his hand—an omen of great destiny among his people—but as a boy, every day of his life was a struggle. His father was dead. He and his mother and brothers were starving.

Temujin's father had been a Mongol chieftain, a leader of one of the many nomadic tribes that herded goats, sheep, and horses across the high steppes of Mongolia. When Temujin's father was poisoned by an enemy band of Tatars, the rest of the family was abandoned by their tribe. Alone in the wilderness, they barely survived. But by the time Temujin was a teen, he had become a leader of men.

Like all the Mongol men, Temujin was an excellent rider. He rode as if he and his horse were one. With a small band of horsemen, Temujin made daring attacks against other tribes and grew to be a powerful and fearless leader. His herds and band grew. He married, but shortly after their marriage his wife, Borte, was captured by enemy Merkit raiders. When

Temujin rescued her months later, his reputation grew even stronger. Over time many families, and then tribes, joined him. His growing forces destroyed his enemies—the Tatars who had poisoned his father, and the Merkits who had stolen his wife. Those who would not submit to him and join his army were killed.

In 1206, Temujin held a great council and called together all of the people of the land. When he raised a white banner showing his emblem of nine horsetails, the crowd cheered. They all agreed that Temujin would be their new leader, and they named him "Very Mighty Lord," or Genghis Khan.

Genghis Khan built a great army, demanding that all the men between the ages of 14 and 60 join him. With his banner raised high, he led his army hundreds of miles to the east. The warriors galloped across wide deserts, sleeping in their saddles and drinking blood from cuts they made in their horses's backs. The walls built by the people of China to protect their towns from invasion were useless against these ferocious raiders. They stormed northern China, conquering millions of people. Then they turned and rode far to the west. They overpowered great empires, destroyed whole cities, and established Genghis Khan as ruler over all.

The Mongol warriors, dressed in leather and steel, would race in on their fast horses to

Genghis Khan on horseback

What's in a Name?

Marco and other Europeans called the Mongols "Tartars," a garbled version of the word Tatar (the tribe whose leader killed Genghis Khan's father). This name sounded like "Tartarus," the ancient Greek name for the lowest regions of hell. To their victims, the ferocious Mongol warriors seemed to be devils from below.

fire a rain of arrows against their enemies. The sight of these sunburnt horsemen galloping in at full speed struck terror in the hearts of millions. They ruthlessly destroyed crops, leaving burning fields in their wake. Cities fell before them, and their citizens were butchered, or enslaved and sent to Mongolia. Before long, their empire stretched from the Black Sea to the Pacific Ocean, from Siberia to the Himalayas.

Genghis Khan died in 1227, while leading his men against a rebellious province of China. After his death, his soldiers leveled whole towns in the province. It is said that every person who saw the funeral procession on its way back to Mongolia was killed, so that none would know of Genghis Khan's death. He was buried secretly and, according to legend, 40 women and 40 horses were sacrificed and buried with him. His tomb has never since been found.

Genghis Khan's empire was divided among his sons and one of his grandsons after his death. One of his sons, Ogodei, became the Great Khan, ruler over all the others. He built a great capital, Karakorum, in the Mongolian homeland. Genghis's grandson, Batu, led a huge army across Russia and into Europe. His army was called the Golden Horde (horde means clan or tribe). Just as Batu was about to lead his Golden Horde on a terrifying raid against Vienna, he received word that the Great

Khan Ogodei had died. Batu withdrew his army from the assault and returned to his homeland to be present when the tribes elected their new leader. Europe was saved.

After Ogodei died, another of Genghis's grandsons, Kublai, became the Great Khan. He conquered the remaining provinces of China and moved his capital from the Mongolian city of Karakorum to a city in northern China. (This was the destination of the Polos' journey.) From here, he ruled the vast Mongol empire.

Though the Mongols were ruthless in battle, they were moderate rulers. They demanded that their subjects pay them in gold, silver, and silk but they allowed the conquered peoples to follow their own customs and religions. Under Mongol rule, towns and roads became safer from bandits. The Mongols even adopted some of the customs of the people they conquered. Kublai Khan adopted the Chinese form of government and conducted Chinese rituals in his palaces.

Everywhere Marco turned, people talked about these new rulers, the Mongols. The great city of Baghdad (in today's Iraq) had long been the most important city of the region. In this noble and immense city, traders grew rich and scholars studied magic, physics, and astronomy. Marco was told that, when the Mongols invaded Baghdad, the Caliph (the city's ruler) had hoarded a huge fortune in gold, silver, and gems. When the Khan saw the Caliph's treasure trove, he scolded him for hoarding the riches. "Why didn't you use your treasure to enlist soldiers and defend your city?" he asked. The Caliph held his tongue. "Since you are so fond of treasure," the Khan said, "I will make you eat it." He locked the Caliph in a high tower with all of his gold and silver until the greedy man starved to death.

Persia

In Persia, the Polos' caravan stopped at Tabriz, a prospering town on the Silk Road. With its beautiful gardens of lush flowers and exotic fruits, Marco thought it the grandest of cities. Its bazaars were crowded with turbaned traders bartering for silk and other fine goods. They haggled in sharp voices over gemstones, fine swords, saddles, and enchantingly beautiful silks with embroidered birds and animals in every color of the rainbow.

Marco learned that Persia (a region we now call Iran) was an ancient land with a history dating back thousands of years. It became a great empire around 550 B.C. under King Cyrus the Great, whose armies conquered much of the Middle East and central Asia. It was said that Cyrus's yellow-robed troops were preceded by swarms of snakes, which sent people and herds stampeding in terror. Cyrus conquered millions, but he met his doom when he led a battle against the nomad queen Tomyris, who chopped off his head!

Colossal Persian bull's head

Say It in Persian

Do you ever wear khaki pants? *Khaki* is a word that came from the Persian language. Play chess? Scholars say the name of this ancient game is from the Persian word *shah*. (They also say the word *checkmate* comes from a Persian phrase meaning "the King is dead.") Say some more in Persian (sometimes referred to as Farsi):

Hello: Salam (*sah-lom*)

Good-bye: Khoda hafez (*ko-da haw-fez*)

Please: Khahesh mikonam (*ko-hesh mik-ko-nam*)

Thank you: Tashakkor mikonam (*tash-a-kor mik-ko-nam*)

Yes: Bale (*bal-leh*)

No: Na (*nah*)

Ruins of Persepolis

The Silk Road

The Polos were not the first to travel the long road between China and the west. Many caravans had followed an ancient path as far back as 200 B.C. Today we call this historic route the Silk Road.

In the distant past, the Chinese had learned the art of making silk from the white fiber of silkworm cocoons. Legend tells that silk was discovered when a cocoon fell into a teacup held by the emperor's wife. When she tried to pick it up, the cocoon unwound in her hand and she drew out the fine, strong thread.

Archaeologists have found silk cloth that was woven almost 5,000 years ago! Only the Chinese knew how to make it, and they kept the knowledge a closely guarded secret. They raised the silkworms on mulberry leaves, then let them spin their cocoons. The cocoons were dropped into hot water and unwound, and the fiber used to make fine cloth. When Chinese traders made contact with cities to the west, they found people willing to pay great prices for silk. Though the route was long and dangerous, there was money to be made.

Long caravans of camels, the only animals that could cross the harsh deserts along the route, carried silk, rhubarb, and pearls to the west. They returned with their packs loaded with gold and gems, perfumes, pomegranates, and nuts. They traveled slowly from oasis to oasis (desert stopovers where water is found). Many of the stopovers grew to be great cities because of the Silk Road traffic.

Goods traveled along the route, and so did people, ideas, and styles of art. Chinese inventions such as gunpowder and the mechanical clock were brought to the west. Buddhism was spread from India to China by monks traveling along the Silk Road. People on both ends of the Road learned about cultures other than their own, and this expanded their ideas about the world.

Trade along the Silk Road was at its greatest between the second century B.C. and the second century A.D. In the seventh century, the road became crowded again, but when the powerful Chinese Tang Dynasty fell in the 10th century, travelers stayed home. The caravans of precious silk, gold, spices, and gemstones were tempting prey for bandits, and only a strong government could keep the road open and safe. When the Mongols came to power, they made the roads safe again for trade. When the Mongol Empire ended, bandits and wars stopped the trade caravans. Merchants found it safer and faster to conduct their trade by sea.

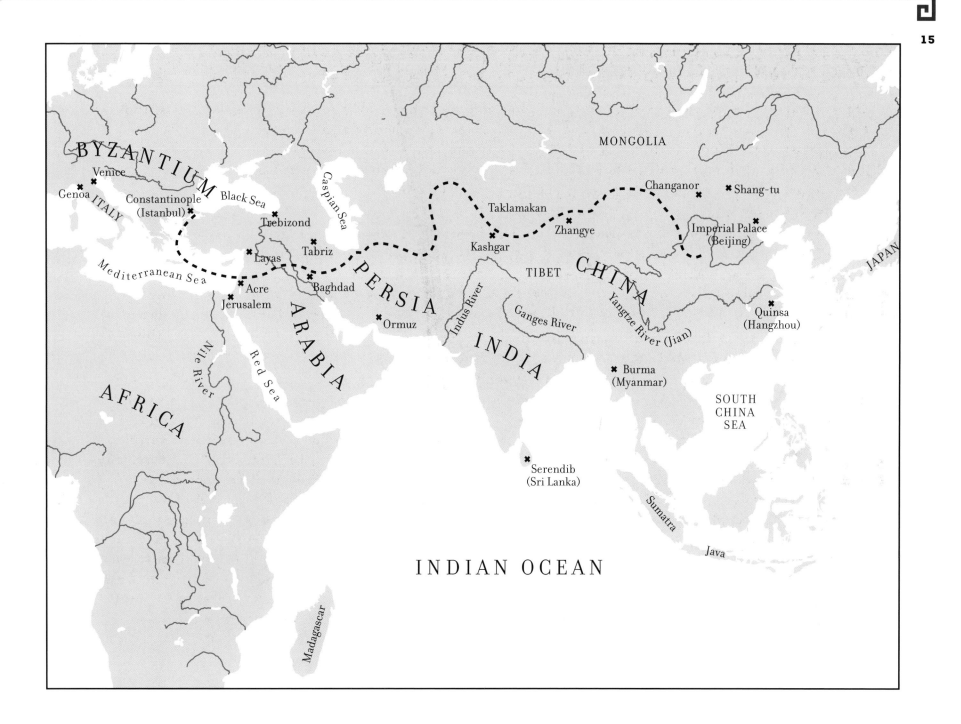

Generations later, when Darius came to power, he ordered his Persian subjects to dig a canal between the Nile and the Red Sea and to build a 1,700-mile-long Royal Road. Darius's couriers raced their chariots along the Royal Road to deliver messages to the king's satraps (governors).

Darius, a great warrior, expanded the kingdom and became ruler of nearly half of the civilized world. To celebrate his triumphs, he ordered the construction of Persepolis. In his awe-inspiring city, the buildings were covered in jewels. The entrance hall of one building was so vast it could hold his 10,000 bodyguards, all young men from the kingdom's finest families. Here Darius sat on his throne to receive gifts—camels and rams, jewelry and carpets—from subjects from every part of his empire. His was the world's greatest empire. It was crushed by the Greek general Alexander the Great, who defeated Darius III and burned Persepolis to the ground.

A century and a half later, a nomadic tribe invaded and conquered Persia. They ruled for hundreds of years until their king was challenged by another tribal leader. The two rulers met in a savage hand-to-hand battle that led to the king's defeat.

The new rulers were called the Sassanian Dynasty (ruling family), and they were mighty

Persian landscape

A Persian Poet

The Moving Finger writes, and having writ,

Moves on: nor all thy Piety nor Wit

Shall lure it back to cancel half a Line,

Nor all thy Tears wash out a Word of it.

These words were written by Omar Khayyam (1048–1131), the great Persian poet who composed "The Rubaiyat." Many people don't know that he was also a mathematician and astronomer. He invented a calendar that needs to be adjusted only one day every 5,000 years—it's more accurate than the calendar we use today.

in battle. With a vast army of thousands mounted on horses, camels, and trumpeting elephants, they vanquished invading Roman troops. Their wealth and power grew. In his great hall, the king sat on a magnificent carpet woven of gold and silver threads. The carpet was designed to look like a beautiful garden, but this garden had thousands of green emeralds for trees, red rubies for flowers, and diamonds for water. The king's golden crown was so heavy with jewels that his head couldn't hold it up—he had to hang the crown from the ceiling with long chains! Under the Sassanian Dynasty, the arts flourished. Great domed and vaulted buildings were created, fine carpets woven, and epic poetry sung. Craftspeople perfected the arts of mosaic and painting in miniature.

The Sassanian Dynasty came to an end when Arab warriors (called *gazi*) overran Persia and cut down the land's armies with the sharp blades of their curved scimitars. The Arabs destroyed the palace of the Persian king and cut his jeweled carpet into pieces. The Arabic rule lasted for three centuries. Then they, too, fell before invading armies. Waves of nomadic tribes invaded from Asia. First came a Turkish tribe led by Alp Arlsan. Alp's mustaches were so long he had to tie them behind his head so they wouldn't get caught in his bowstring!

Genghis Khan's hordes followed and devastated Persia. His armies destroyed five cities, killing every resident down to the last dog and cat. One of his grandsons, Hulegu, continued the carnage, massacring tens of thousands. After Hulegu's death, his brother Kublai became the Khan in 1265, just six years before Marco's journey.

One day the Polos' caravan came to the Castle of the Fire Worshippers. The people who lived here were followers of an ancient religion called Zorastrianism. They kept a sacred fire constantly burning, Marco said, and "adored that fire as a god and made all their sacrifices with it." The founder of their religion, Zoroaster, preached that people must choose good over evil, light over darkness. The fire they kept represented goodness and light. Marco was told that the Three Wise Men were buried at the castle.

Land of Many Religions

Marco had been brought up as a Christian, so he knew the story of Jesus' birth, when the Three Wise Men followed a star to Bethlehem to find a newborn baby boy. The child, Jesus, learned his father's trade as a carpenter, but when he grew up, he became a teacher. With a group of followers, Jesus traveled throughout the countryside, teaching people a new way of life. He performed healing miracles, and some began to say he was the deliverer whose coming had been predicted since ancient times. Jesus' teachings of love and compassion upset those who were in power, and he was jailed, tortured, and crucified. After his death, his followers continued to spread his word. Soon his teachings and the story of his life, death, and resurrection (revival from death) were written in books called the Gospels. Over time, the Christian religion was founded on Jesus' life and teachings.

Zoroastrianism, which had much in common with Christianity, had been the main religion of the Persian people for a very long time. When the Arabic armies invaded Persia, that ancient religion was replaced by the Arab one—Islam.

Islam was based on the visions received by Muhammad, a modest trader from the city of Mecca. Muhammad had lost his parents when he was only a child and was brought up by his uncle, who was a merchant. As a young boy, Muhammad was a shepherd who stayed with his flocks of sheep out in the country for weeks at a time. He grew up and married and followed in his uncle's trade, but still he loved to go off by himself to meditate and think. One day, while deep in thought, Muhammad heard the

Ramadan and Eidul-Fitr

Ramadan is a sacred month in the Islamic religion. During this period, Muslims fast (go without food) from dawn to sunset every day. They fast to glorify Allah, to understand what it's like to be poor and hungry, and to discipline themselves physically and spiritually. At the end of the month they celebrate Eidul-Fitr, the Festival of Fastbreaking, a day with special food, visits to friends and relatives, and presents for children.

voice of the angel Gabriel, who instructed him to tell his people to obey the will of God (Allah).

Over the next 22 years, Muhammad received Allah's word. He became known as a prophet (one who delivers divine messages). The teachings he received were laid out in a sacred text called the Koran. They outlined five basic duties for Islam's followers (who are called Muslims): to declare their faith, to pray five times a day, to share with those less fortunate, to fast during the month of Ramadan, and to make a pilgrimage to the holy city of Mecca

Traditions in Common

Sometimes it's easier to notice the differences between people, but if we look with an open mind, we can see many things in common. Christianity and Islam are very much alike, and they both have roots in Judaism, an ancient religion dating back thousands of years.

All three religions have holy books that tell their stories and traditions. The Muslim Koran, the Christian Bible, and the Jewish Torah all tell the stories of Adam and Eve, Noah's Ark, and the ancient prophets. All three religions believe in bodily resurrection. All three observe holy days and periods of fasting (the Muslims during Ramadan, the Christians during Lent, and the Jews on Yom Kippur). Though they call him by different names, Christians, Jews, and Muslims all believe in the same God.

once in their lifetimes. Those who obeyed Allah's commands would be rewarded with an eternity in paradise.

✖ ✖ ✖

Marco's caravan came to a high desert—land too harsh and dry for their horses. Only camels could survive the rest of the trip. Soon the caravan's long line of camels began the desert crossing, their packsaddles stuffed with supplies. Days passed without a village in sight. When the travelers spotted an oasis on the horizon, their hearts rose at the thought of cool water and rest under the shade of palm trees. It took weeks before they arrived at the desert's end. Here a once-powerful city stood guard at the border of a great plain. Within its walls were gardens and orchards, but it was nearly empty of people, a result of Mongol attacks.

After the desert crossing, this land looked like paradise to Marco. Trees heavy with dates and pomegranates surrounded the city. Turtle doves and partridges ate from their branches. Out in the fields, farmers drove humped oxen as white as snow. Hungry Marco wrote about rams "as big as donkeys, fine and fat and good to eat."

The city was surrounded by high walls that protected its remaining people from marauding bandits. The townspeople suffered at the hands of bandits who prowled the countryside. Marco claimed these bandits worked a powerful spell before their attacks—making the day dark as night so that none could see them coming. Actually, the attackers did not practice magic but they were very shrewd. They advanced during windstorms, so their attacks would be disguised by the windblown dust and sand. They were upon their victims before they could be seen.

The Polos left the city and moved across the plain. One day a fierce windstorm blew. Out of the swirling darkness came a pack of howling bandits! Men and camels scattered. Marco and his father and uncle raced across the sands until they came to a fortress where they found protection. Many of their fellow travelers were captured, taken prisoner, or killed by the bandits.

It took courage to continue their journey with bandits and murderers lying in wait for unwary travelers. But the Polos would not let the threat of danger discourage them; they were soon on their way again. They traveled to the city of Ormuz, a bustling port city on the Persian Gulf, where they hoped to find a ship to continue their journey by sea. Like Marco's home in Venice, Ormuz was a trading center. The merchants here were from faraway countries unknown to Marco. The ships in the ports were loaded with spices, gold cloth, and pearls.

One Hump or Two?

The camels of Marco Polo's caravan were the Bactrian, or two-humped variety. Like the larger Arabian Dromedary (the one-humped camel), these animals are perfectly adapted for the desert, where temperatures range from 100° F to -20° F. They can close their nostrils against wind-blown dust and sand. Bony ridges above their eyes provide shade from the burning sun, and long lashes and a special, thin membrane protect their eyes from sand. The camel's two-toed feet are broad and flat. By spreading out over a greater surface area, they prevent the animal from sinking in sand.

Most important for life in the desert, the camel can live for long periods without water. Because it doesn't sweat in high temperatures, it doesn't lose precious bodily fluids. The camel can live weeks without water, but, when it comes to an oasis, clear out—it can drink more than 20 gallons in 10 minutes! It also carries its own food supply. The camel's hump is fatty tissue that the animal draws on when food is scarce. As the fat is used up, the hump gets smaller.

Even within the city's walls, the Polos were not safe. While they were there, Ormuz came under attack from an army, thousands strong, from a neighboring province. But just as the army came close, the wind began to blow. Soon sand and dust flew in a ferocious desert gale (called a *simoom*). When the wind stopped there was not a soldier to be seen! They had been buried beneath the sands.

The people of Ormuz knew how dangerous these storms could be. "Quite often during the summer, a sandstorm is whipped up by a wind so hot that it would kill anyone who was not warned in time," Marco wrote. Everyone would rush to a nearby river and submerge themselves in water up to their necks to protect themselves from the heat and sand.

No one wept for the enemy soldiers, but the people of Ormuz held long mourning rituals when one of their own died. Once a day for four years, widows wailed loudly for their husbands. When they got tired, they hired someone else to do their wailing for them. "There are women in this country who are so good at crying," Marco wrote, "that for a price, they will cry for any length of time beside anyone's grave."

The ships in the ports of Ormuz were "of the worst kind, and dangerous for navigation." They were simply planks held together with coconut fiber. Marco's father and uncle, experienced sailors, shuddered at the thought of setting sail in the ragged boats. The Polos decided to leave Ormuz and continue their journey over land.

Make a Mosaic

Persian artists used bits of tile or glass to make their designs. You can buy these supplies at craft stores. Mosaics can also be made from pebbles, stones, and seashells. Collect things from outdoors or raid the kitchen for "ingredients" for this mosaic.

What you need

Newspaper

Pencil

Paper

Selection of mosaic pieces, including

    Dried beans, seeds, and pastas of different colors and shapes

    Pieces of broken buttons

    Pebbles, stones, small seashells

    Mosaic tiles from a craft store

    Bits of aluminum foil

Paste

Shallow container (such as a lid from a coffee can)

Tweezers

$1/2$ cup water

Large paper cup

1 cup plaster of paris

Stirring stick

Sponge

Dry rag

1 Spread newspaper out over your workspace. Draw your design first on a piece of paper, keeping in mind that your design will have to fit into your shallow container, then practice arranging the mosaic pieces such as beans, stones, tiles, and other objects on top of the design.

2 Spread paste in a thick layer over the bottom of the shallow container. Using tweezers, carefully place the mosaic pieces on top of the paste the same way you placed them over your design. Leave a little space around each piece. Let dry for a few hours.

3 Pour the water into the paper cup. Pour plaster of paris into the water by sifting the powder through your fingers. Let the mixture sit for 5 minutes, then stir with a stick until it is thick and soupy. Slowly pour the mixture over your mosaic so that it seeps down into the spaces between the pieces.

4 Let it rest for 5 minutes, then wipe the mosaic with a damp sponge. Let it dry overnight. Then dust off the excess plaster with a dry rag.

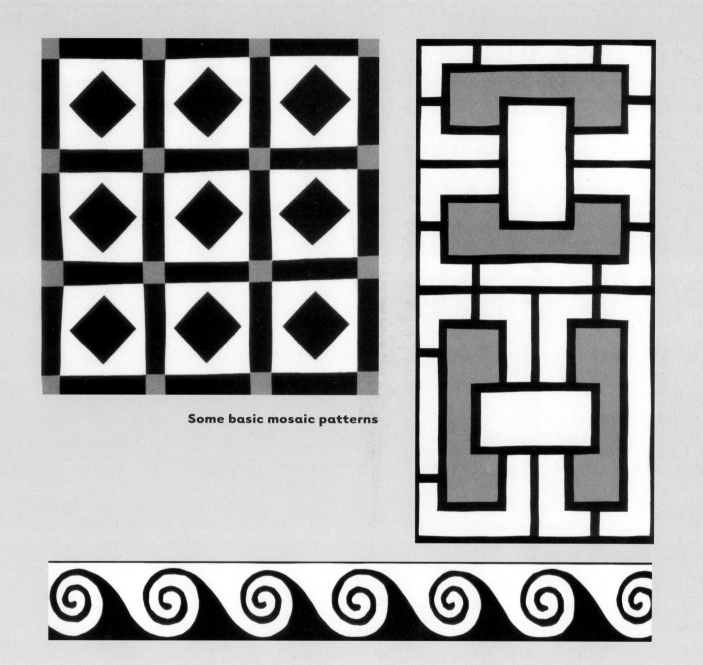

Some basic mosaic patterns

The Great Wall of China

2 In the Realm of Kublai Khan

After days spent crossing a barren, dry desert, drowning at sea didn't seem so bad. They'd had no water since they'd left Ormuz, and there was not a single home or village in sight. Finally, with great relief, the travelers reached a spring of cool water emerging from a deep cavern. Here they rested and drank deeply before continuing on their way.

Soon they came to a large plain covered with trees, the only green place they'd seen for 100 miles. The caravan stopped and the Polos replenished their supplies at a nearby town. The villagers told Marco how lucky he was that the Old Man of the Mountains was no longer alive.

Near this place, the Old Man once lived with his murderous gang in a secret valley stronghold. No one was safe from them. Shahs, caliphs, and crusaders were killed in their own palaces at the Old Man's bidding. Even the kings of faraway England and France feared him. The Mongolian ruler Khakhan Mangu, though he had a bodyguard of 500 soldiers,

went into hiding when he heard that 100 disguised men from the Old Man of the Mountains had been sent to kill him.

According to the villagers, the Old Man convinced his followers that his valley stronghold was Paradise. First, he had men drugged and brought to the valley. When they awoke, they were treated to every delight in a beautiful garden oasis where the trees dripped with fruit and the rivers sang. He drugged them again and brought them out of the valley, telling them that only by doing his will would they be allowed to re-enter and stay in Paradise. They obeyed his every wish. Once, when showing off his gang's loyalty to a visitor, the Old Man signaled to some guards standing on a tower. At his gesture, they all jumped hundreds of feet to their deaths.

No one could attack them in their protected valley stronghold, even though many had tried. Finally, after a two-year siege, they were defeated by the Mongols. Before this time, the gang had so terrified the world that their name, Assassin, became the word for a person who kills secretly or treacherously.

Afghanistan

Grateful that the Assassins no longer existed, the Polos left the town on a path to the north and east. They were leaving Persia on a route that would take them over treacherous mountains into Asia. Lions inhabited this wild country (Marco wrote that they were uncommonly large and very numerous!). They passed mountains of white salt, and mountains rich with fine rubies and lapis lazuli. The men of one country wore animal skins and turbans. In a neighboring country, the women padded their bottoms with cloth, for those with the widest hips were thought to be the most beautiful. The finest breed of horses in the world was found here, each animal marked with a white blaze on its forehead. Swift falcons nested in the lofty

Marco Polo's Sheep

Six hundred years after Marco described the huge sheep, the animals were discovered by scientists and named *Ovis poli* in his honor. Also called argali, they're the world's largest wild sheep, standing four feet high at the shoulder and weighing up to 350 pounds. Near extinction, they live in remote mountainous regions of Asia.

mountains. Shepherds made their summer homes in caves and herded their sheep in the high mountain meadows.

The long journey took a toll on Marco and he fell ill. His father and his uncle were gravely concerned. They brought the caravan to a halt; the young man was quickly failing. The Polos delayed their journey for nearly a year while Marco recovered. The pure mountain streams and clear air of the pleasant country helped to make him well again.

When Marco was strong enough to travel, they continued on their way. A great wilderness lay ahead, and they had loaded their animals with extra supplies and food. Every day, the path climbed higher and higher into the mountains. With snow-covered peaks on every side, Marco thought they had reached the highest land in the world. Below them lay the foothills, a large lake, and a crystal-clear river flowing into the distance over a grassy plain. Wild sheep grazed on the mountains' slopes, the males standing guard over the herds.

They were now on the high plains of Pamir, the "Roof of the World." Along the path, shepherds had piled mounds of antlers, horns, and bones. These were shrines that also served to mark the trail when it was covered deep with snow. The Polos were 15,000 feet above sea level, in a land so inhospitable that there were no villages, and so high that no birds flew there. When they lit their campfire at night, Marco noticed that the fire did not give off much heat.

This country of steep mountains, treeless plains, and cruel desert wastelands was not a very inviting place, but it had been fought over countless times by people anxious to control the ancient silk trade route. The Persian king Cyrus the Great held it for a time. Alexander the Great brought his armies over these mountains and

Translation, please!

So many different kinds of people have lived in Afghanistan that today more than 70 different languages are spoken in this small country!

married the local satrap's daughter, Roxana. After Alexander's rule ended, nomadic tribes took over the land. Rulers from India pushed into the region, bringing with them a new religion—Buddhism. In the first century, the Chinese invaded; in the seventh, Arab gazi warriors pushed them back. Genghis Khan's Mongols overthrew the Arab rule, leaving a path of destruction thousands of miles long. Tamerlane was the last of the Mongol conquerors. He established his capital in this land, which we know today as Afghanistan. This capital, Herat, became a great city of learning, trade, and culture.

It took nearly two months to cross these mountains (the Hindu Kush). The narrow valleys were thick with vegetation, which slowed their every step. It took long days to struggle up the steep mountain slopes. They forded swift, rocky rivers, and followed the trail through forests of cedar and pine. Snow leopards, bears, wolves, ibex (wild goats), and markhors (mountain sheep) lived in these mountains. It seemed as if there was no end to their journey. At every peak, they paused to look ahead, and saw range after range of mountains. Finally, one day they began a long descent. Ahead in the distance lay the city of Kashgar.

Kashgar was exotic and exciting, especially after months in the mountain wilderness. Even in Marco's time, it was an ancient city. People from east, west, north, and south came to haggle and trade in open-air markets. Turbaned merchants hawked their wares—silk, melons, jades, furs, and fine, fat sheep. Dark-haired Mongols bartered for horses and touched the ground when the bargain was struck (a sign of their good word). Color and noise and the smell of roasting mutton replaced the quiet existence on the Roof of the World.

China

The Polos had entered the realm of Kublai Khan. His palace was still a thousand miles to the east, but his influence reached far. As their caravan moved from Kashgar to Kotan, Charchan to Lop, Marco met the Khan's subjects and heard stories about the great ruler.

As always, Marco kept his eyes and ears open. During the months of travel, he had mastered several languages so he could speak with the people he met. The inhabitants of this country spoke a language he'd never heard before. It was hard to form the strange words and phrases. He noticed their clothes, customs, and food. In one city, the people practiced an unusual marriage custom: if a man left home for more than 20 days, his wife had the right to take a new husband. The people of Charchan, which bordered on a sandy desert, were wary of invaders. If they got word of approaching bandits, they took their families and animals out into the desert, to secret oases where they could hide until the danger past.

The Polos lingered in the town of Lop to gather supplies. Ahead of them was the most dangerous part of their journey—the Takla Makan. This was a wide, barren desert that held only 20 small oases where they could obtain water and rest. "To travel the length of it would be a vain attempt," Marco wrote, as it would take nearly a year to cross. The Polos planned a route across its narrowest point, but this would still require 30 dangerous days. They made sure their camels were well fed and rested, and stocked up on all necessities before setting out.

Thirst and starvation were not the only dangers of the desert, according to the people of Lop. They warned Marco of evil spirits, too. "Don't lag behind the caravan," they told him,

What's in a Name?

China took its name from Emperor Shihuangdi, who was from the province of Qin (or Ch'in). Today, we know the country as the People's Republic of China. Marco Polo called it Cathay. The ancient Chinese called their country the Middle Kingdom, because they believed it was the center of the earth.

The Kingdom of Prester John

Europeans believed that somewhere in central Asia a Christian monarch named Prester John ruled over a vast kingdom. A rumor began that this king would come to Europe to aid the knights of the Crusades. Copies of a letter this king had reportedly sent to the Pope spread throughout Europe. "I am Prester John," it said, "the greatest monarch under heaven. Seventy-two kings pay tribute to me, and all the wild beasts and monstrous creatures are in my domain. My dominion reaches through the desert toward the place of the rising sun. When I go to war, 13 great crosses of gold and jewels are carried before me, each one followed by 10,000 knights and 100,000 footmen. In my marvelous castle is a marvelous mirror in which I see everything that goes on in my kingdom. My domain holds the fountain of youth and pebbles which make their possessor invisible. There are ants which dig gold, fish which make the royal purple dye, and the salamander which lives in fire."

When Marco discovered Christians in central Asia, he believed he was in Prester John's kingdom. He never saw any gold-digging ants or the castle with the marvelous mirror. He found people making asbestos cloth that could pass unharmed through fire, but "of the salamander supposed to exist in fire, I could never discover any trace."

The kingdom of Prester John was a myth, but it may have been based on truth. Some scholars think he may have been a Mongol leader who had converted to Christianity. In later centuries, Prester John's mythical kingdom was believed to be in Ethiopia.

"for as soon as the last camel is out of your sight, the spirits will call your name." They claimed that the spirits used the voices of loved ones to lure unwary travelers off the path. Haunting music or the sounds of beating drums and clashing weapons led men astray. The people also spoke of mirages, images of fantastic armies and castles that appeared on distant horizons. With these warnings ringing in their ears, the Polos set out from Lop.

It would be easy to fall behind, put into a trance by the rhythm of the saddle and the deadly sameness of the landscape. The Polos were very careful to keep on the path from oasis to oasis. They attached bells to their camels. If someone strayed, they could follow the sound of the ringing bells. Each person in the caravan knew that day's destination and path. The moaning of the wind over the dry sand sounded like a mournful voice to Marco. But all the members of the caravan stayed vigilant against the dangers and safely crossed the forbidding desert.

It was with great relief that they reached the towns on the opposite side of the Takla Makan. Here, wedged between the broad desert and fiery red mountains, the people had solved the problem of desert life by constructing ingenious underground channels, hundreds of miles long, to bring water from the mountain slopes to irrigate their crops. Nomads lived in these red mountains. They often swooped down to attack traders following the Silk Road, which here skirted the Mongolian steppes on its way to the cities of China.

Marco was surprised to find all sorts of religions practiced here, including Buddhism, Christianity, and Islam. Some of the people worshiped animal spirits and sacrificed rams to their gods in honor of the birth of a child. At funerals, they offered food and drink to the corpse, to fortify it for its journey to the next world, and they sent it off by playing every musical instrument in the city—"an incessant din!" Marco exclaimed.

Marco found monasteries that housed thousands of Buddhist monks carved into cliff faces. The cave monasteries were crowded with statues of the Buddha, carved of wood and stone and plated with gold. The walls of the caves were covered with paintings of the Buddha.

Buddhism

Buddhist monks had traveled along the Silk Road from India, bringing with them the teachings and practices of their religion. They taught the Chinese people about Siddhartha, who had been born a prince in a fabulous

Buddha (Maravijaya Buddha)

palace. Siddhartha's family protected him as a boy from seeing anything painful or sad and did not allow him outside the palace grounds. One day, he left the palace and saw for the first time people who were poor, sick, old, and dying. Siddhartha was shocked. He decided to devote his life to finding the reason for such suffering.

Siddhartha gave up his wealth and his family to wander throughout the countryside. After traveling many miles and seeking for many years, he sat beneath a fig tree to meditate. While in a deep trance, Siddhartha reached enlightenment. He saw and understood the meaning of suffering and of life and death. Because he reached enlightenment, he received the name of the Buddha (the Enlightened One).

The Buddha's followers practiced meditation and shared his vision with others. Buddhism became one of the major religions of China. The monks taught that each person could reach Nirvana (freedom from suffering and death) by following the Eightfold Path of meditation and self-discipline. Only by learning to rid oneself of desire could the Buddhist break the cycle of suffering. This goal could take many lifetimes (Buddhists believe in reincarnation—the rebirth of the soul into another body and a new life).

* * *

The Polos found the trading good in one city (today's Zhangye) and stayed there for a very long time. Marco wandered through its markets and streets and visited its temples. Built into the city's walls were tall watchtowers, where, in previous years, sentries had stood scanning the horizon for barbarian invaders. Not far from here was the city of Karakorum, which until recently had been the capital of the Mongolian empire. Marco remarked that this city was surrounded by a tall, wide wall of earth.

China's First Emperor

In ancient times, before China was a united country, small cities throughout Asia had built such walls to keep themselves safe from invasion. In the third century B.C. Emperor Shihuangdi rose to power, united six independent, warring regions into one huge country—China—and ordered his subjects to build a Great Wall.

He had set out ahead of his troops to conquer a neighboring province when he was only 13 years old. Twenty-five years later, he was Emperor of China. The Emperor ruled from an imperial compound made up of hundreds of residences, harems, and treasuries spread out

The Great Wall of China

over 70 miles. In a show of pride, he erected buildings that were replicas of the palaces of kings he had conquered. The buildings were connected by secret passageways so the Emperor could keep his whereabouts hidden. He never slept in the same place twice.

Emperor Shihuangdi divided the country into provinces. Each province was governed by civil servants (officials who had passed a series of rigorous examinations established by the

Did Marco See the Great Wall?

Over centuries, the first Great Wall deteriorated. After Marco Polo's time, during the Ming Dynasty (1368–1644), the Chinese people set to work rebuilding the wall. What remains of the Great Wall of China today are the sections rebuilt during the Ming Dynasty. This Wall is 1,600 miles long, approximately 24 feet high, and so wide that eight people can walk side by side along its top. Stone watchtowers loom every 300 to 600 feet. The Great Wall is so big that it can be seen from space!

Marco described large walls of earth and fortifications around towns, but didn't mention the Great Wall in his story. Some scholars believe this means he never traveled all the way to China. Others have pointed out that most of the first Great Wall had deteriorated by the time of Marco's journey.

There are questions about other parts of Marco's story, too. Marco never mentioned the Chinese practice of footbinding. (Small feet on women were considered beautiful. Wealthy Chinese families tightly wrapped the feet of their baby girls to keep their feet from growing.) Some scholars say this is proof that Marco was never in China. Others say the practice may not have been common in the parts of China Marco visited and that he may not have been allowed to see the women of wealthy families because they did not leave their homes. Marco also does not mention acupuncture (a Chinese medical treatment that uses needles) or teahouses or the Chinese practice of fishing with birds called cormorants. The many details Marco gives about the way people in China lived have convinced other scholars that his story is true.

Emperor). He abolished the different systems for weights and measures each region had used and made everyone use the same system. He established laws and ordered the people to use a common written language. His workers built roads, bridges, and canals.

The Emperor's biggest worry was an invasion from the north. He ordered his people to link together the different walls of the widespread towns to make one Great Wall. Hundreds of thousands of his subjects got to work. They piled up wide mounds of earth and covered the mounds with stones. They built tall watchtowers from which sentries could watch for approaching enemies. Some of the workers were crushed beneath stones or fell while building the tall structures. Their bodies were hastily buried beneath the wall and the others kept working. After 14 years, their work was complete, and the 3,000-mile-long wall (called "The Serpent Made of Stone") snaked from one end of the kingdom to the other.

Emperor Shihuangdi was very cruel. He taxed his people so heavily they could barely survive. His laws were strict and the penalties harsh. He had his soldiers burn every text they could find, and even ordered them to bury hundreds of scholars alive! After his death, the people of China revolted against his government. The peasant who led the revolt became

The Qin Emperor's Tomb

In 1974, laborers digging a well near the city of Xian came upon the 2,200-year-old tomb of the Qin Emperor. They had uncovered one of the century's most amazing archeological finds.

The dead emperor's tomb was guarded by more than 6,000 life-sized terra cotta warriors. Each warrior was created with an individual face and body. Some were fat, some thin, some had mustaches, some wore special armor. Some appeared to march. Others knelt with their bows ready to shoot. Terra cotta horses pulled terra cotta chariots.

Seven hundred thousand workmen spent 34 years making the tomb of Qin Emperor Shihuangdi. When the emperor died, his concubines and servants, along with many of the artisans who built his tomb, were buried with him. Stone gates closed on the dead and the living. The tomb was defended with hidden darts and concealed crossbows set to shoot at unsuspecting prowlers and explorers.

Detail of terra cotta warriors

the next emperor, the first of the Han Dynasty. Emperor Shihuangdi's empire ended and his Great Wall fell into disrepair.

The crumbling remains of the first Great Wall meant nothing to Genghis Khan's hordes. They broke through and invaded China. One town after another fell under their piercing arrows! They burned crops and villages, leaving a smoking wasteland in their wake. Now his descendants ruled this land and countries thousands of miles to the south and west.

Kitchen Terra Cotta

Terra cotta ("cooked earth") is clay mixed with sand, then baked after molding. Qin artisans made 6,000 terra cotta warriors to guard Emperor Shihuangdi's tomb. You can make miniature warriors from clay mixed in your own kitchen.

Adult supervision required

What you need

Oven

1¼ cups boiling water

Pot

1 cup salt

Spoon

2 cups flour

Bowl

Cutting board

Red and orange food coloring

4 tablespoons paprika

Toothpicks

Cheese grater

Cookie sheet

1 Preheat the oven to 250° F. Boil the water in the pot, then stir in the salt. Place the flour in the bowl. Pour the salt water into the flour and mix with the spoon. Divide into four pieces.

2 Place one piece on the cutting board and drip 8 drops of yellow and 4 drops of red food coloring onto it. Sprinkle with 1 tablespoon paprika. Knead until the color is distributed, then shape the clay into soldiers, horses, or evil emperors! (Some tips: Roll pieces of clay into balls to make heads and eyes. Roll out clay "worms" for legs and arms. You can use toothpicks to carve details. Push a piece of clay through a cheese grater to make hair.)

3 Repeat with other pieces. Place the finished pieces on the cookie sheet, put them in the oven, and bake for 2 hours, until dry.

Mongol Life

Marco learned as much as he could about the Mongols, for he knew that soon he would meet their leader, Kublai Khan. He learned that the Mongols were a nomadic people from central Asia. They traveled with the seasons, seeking grass for their horses and other animals (sheep, goats, camels, and yaks). Extended families (a man with his many wives, siblings, and children) lived in large, round tents called *gers*. The *gers* were made of cross-hatched willow branches covered with felt. Each was set up so that its door faced the rising sun. Guests were always welcome to join a family in its *ger* and were given a seat of honor opposite the door. When it was time to move (as often as four times a year), the *gers* and other belongings were piled on carts pulled by yaks, and the tribe made its way to a new location.

The proud Mongol men loved best to hunt. They trained hawks to hunt for them. The great birds flew, killed their prey, and returned to perch on the arms of their trainers. The Mongols raided and fought with other tribes and settled peoples. When they rode great distances, they carried dried meat and curds in their packsaddles and ate as they rode. When they ran out of food, they drank the blood of

Drink Up!

If you ever find yourself offered *airag* in a Mongol's *ger*, drink three bowls of it or you'll offend your host.

their horses. Their favorite drink was bitter-tasting *airag* (fermented mare's milk).

At home on the Mongolian steppes, they held great contests with competitions in wrestling, archery, and horsemanship. They played a fierce game on horseback in which they fought over the carcass of a calf. The women prepared meals and made clothing, shoes, and *gers*. They took care of all the trading and selling. They even watched over the herds. Each man had many wives, with the first wife ranking highest in importance in the household. When a man's father died, he married all the wives his father left behind, except for the woman who was his own mother.

When a baby was born, the family held a special ceremony. The baby was bathed in meat broth and given a name in honor of a special recent event. (Genghis Khan was

A Warrior Princess

Marco heard a legend about a Mongol chieftain's daughter who was strong and brave and fiercely independent. The beautiful Khutulun loved to ride, hunt, and wrestle—and didn't want to settle down. She refused to marry unless she met her match. She challenged the men of her country to feats of strength and skill. Any opponent who lost to her had to give her 100 horses. The winner could have her hand in marriage.

Many young men took up the challenge, and one after another lost. Soon Khutulun had 10,000 horses! One day, a wealthy and handsome young man came to challenge the princess. He bet 1,000 horses against her hand in marriage that he could win a wrestling match against Khutulun. Khutulun's parents, who very much wished that their daughter would marry, told her to let the young prince win. The whole tribe watched as the opponents fought. First the prince, then the princess seemed to be winning. The combatants fought with all their strength. Finally, Khutulun threw the prince to the ground in triumph.

Khutulun never married. She rode and fought at her father's side as his greatest and bravest warrior.

named Temujin because right before his birth his father had defeated a rival Mongol leader by that name.) Mongol girls made elaborate headdresses and embroidered colorful designs of trees, birds, and animals on felt to decorate the *gers*. Boys learned to hunt and spent long winter days playing a version of hockey with a puck made from a camel's anklebone. Parents arranged marriages for their children, sending gifts and poems back and forth between the *gers* of the two families.

The Mongol people felt there was a sacred spirit in everything in nature, from the wide blue skies of their native land to the fire that warmed them at night. Each household had a god that looked over its family and herds. The family offered food to this god at every meal and also poured some of the broth from their meat outside their door as an offering to other gods. The dances and chants of their shamans (medicine men) encouraged the spirits to bring healing to their people. As they encountered other people, some of the Mongols converted to new religions.

Their land was harsh and unforgiving, a high plateau country bordered by mountains and desert. It taught them how to make do with very little. Their herds supplied all of their needs, from mutton dinners to sheepskin coats. Even their bows were made of yak horns

Yogurt—Breakfast of Warriors

The nomadic Mongols didn't raise crops. All their food came from their herds of animals. They had their choice of boiled mutton, dried mutton, or roasted mutton every day! The women churned milk to make cheese, curds, airag, and yogurt. Here's an easy way to make yogurt at home.

Adult supervision required

What you need

3 cups water

Saucepan

Stovetop

Kitchen thermometer

Clean glass quart jar with a lid

1 cup powdered milk

3 tablespoons plain yogurt (use a brand
   containing live and active cultures)

Insulated lunch bag

Blanket

1 Heat the water in a saucepan on the stovetop to 130° F and pour it into the quart jar. Add the powdered milk, screw on the lid, and shake up the mixture. Open the jar and add the yogurt. Replace the lid and mix thoroughly.

2 Place the jar in an insulated lunch bag, then wrap the bag in a blanket. Let it sit for 10–20 hours, until the yogurt is thick. Keep in refrigerator.

Nomadic Mongols moving camp

and sinews. A Mongol child learned to ride a horse almost before he or she could walk, and a man's horses were his greatest possession. Anyone caught stealing a horse was cut in two with a sword, unless he was able to pay nine times the value of the stolen animal.

Genghis Khan's conquests spread members of his tribe to countries from Persia to China. Still, when any of the chiefs died, they were brought all the way to the steppes for their funeral. Huge caravans accompanied by thousands of horsemen brought their bodies to a

Hold the Musk!

Marco described the musk deer as a cross between a goat and an antelope. They aren't goats or antelopes, but they're not deer either (because they don't grow antlers). Scientists have placed the musk deer in a family of its own.

Musk deer are one of the smallest hoofed mammals, weighing only 20 to 25 pounds. The males grow tusks ("as white as ivory," Marco said). These small, delicate animals are only found in Asia. They're very secretive and come out to graze in the dark of evening or early morning. Their brown, speckled coloring serves as camouflage. They need all the protection they can get, for they are heavily hunted. The musk deer has a gland that produces a brown, waxy substance that people use to make fine perfumes and soaps. It is worth five times its weight in gold. Synthetic musk is available, and only its use can save the musk deer from extinction.

secret place in the Altai Mountains of Mongolia. Anyone who happened to see the body of a Mongol chieftain on its way to its burial place was sacrificed to attend him in the next world.

Eventually, it was time for the Polos' caravan to move on. They were very near now to the palace of the Khan. In the meantime, everything was so strange and exciting! The people looked different. The men Marco met here had straight, dark hair and beardless faces. And the animals! Marco saw white camels decorated with bells and ribbons, and huge yaks pulling plows across the fields. He saw musk deer, valued for their musk-producing glands, and beautiful pheasants with tail feathers as long as his arm.

One day they came to a beautiful place that Marco called Changanor. They learned that the Khan often visited here when he wanted to hunt and relax in the country. His keepers stocked the forests and lakes with game and birds. Cranes, swans, fat pheasants, and quail were numerous and so tame that they would appear when the keepers whistled.

In Changanor, the Polos were met by couriers sent by Kublai Khan. The Khan had been told that the Polos were near, and it was his wish that they hurry to his court. It had been years since Niccolo and Maffeo left his palace, and he was very eager to see his Italian visitors again. He ordered his couriers to escort the Polos to his summer palace, and instructed the people in towns along their path to give the travelers every comfort. It took 40 more days of travel, but as guests of the Khan they enjoyed fine foods and luxurious lodgings along the way. Finally, after three and a half years and 6,000 miles, they reached their destination. Before them was Shang-tu. The Khan was waiting.

Say It in Mongol

The English word *horde*, meaning a pack or swarm, came from the Mongol word *orda* (which means a camp). The Mongols also gave us the name of the Gobi Desert (*gobi* is the Mongol word for "desert"). Here are a few other Mongol words to add to your vocabulary.

Hello: Sajng banjou (*sang ban-joo*)

Good-bye: Bayartaj (*bay-are-tag*)

Please: Ajaamuu (*a-ja-moo*)

Thank you: Bayarlalaa (*bay-are-lay-la*)

Yes: Dza (*za*)

No: Ügüi (*u-gwee*)

Marco Polo welcomed at the court of Kublai Khan

3 Dragons and Dynasties

Hundreds of eyes followed them as the Polos were escorted to the Khan's chambers. The supreme ruler's officials and servants lined the courtyards and hallways of the Khan's summer palace at Shang-tu. They watched and wondered—who were these strangers? Marco and his father and uncle were brought before Kublai Khan, ruler of empires, sovereign to millions. The three kowtowed (bowed so low that their foreheads touched the ground) and waited for him to speak.

The Khan was 60 years old but stout and strong. His fine silk robes shimmered, and his black eyes snapped. "Rise," he said, "and tell me everything about your journey." He listened attentively as Marco's father and uncle related the tale of their many adventures. They presented him with the letters and gifts of crystal from the Pope and the precious oil from the Holy Sepulchre that they had carried by ship, horse, and camel all the way from the Holy Land. He held it reverently, then passed it to one of his attendants, instructing him to find a safe place for it. He turned to Marco, then back to the boy's father. "And who is this boy?"

the Khan asked. "My son," said Niccolo, "and your servant."

"He is welcome," said Kublai Khan. "His service shall please me much." He placed the Polos in seats of honor at his table and called for a great feast to welcome these guests from distant lands.

The Polos stayed at the Khan's palace as his esteemed guests. Marco quickly absorbed the language and customs of the court. He learned everything he could about the Khan and his kingdom.

Kublai Khan commanded the empire won by his grandfather, Genghis Khan. His father and jugglers. The royal magician, with a wave of one hand, caused cups to fly from one table to another. When the mighty Khan lifted his cup to drink, everyone fell to their knees, and musicians played until he set the cup on the table once again.

The summer residence of Shang-tu was surrounded by an outer city and protected behind tall earthen walls. Just outside the Khan's marble palace was a royal park of large forests and rich meadows stocked with wild deer, boar, and goats. In the center of the park was a huge pavilion. Its tall columns were carved into the shapes of dragons, the symbol of the emperor. Its roof was made of gilded bamboo cane. The columns were held to the ground by 200 strong silk cords. This pavilion could be taken apart and moved, like the nomadic Mongol's *ger*, wherever the Khan desired.

The Khan spent the warm summer months hunting and hawking at Shang-tu. Here he kept a stable of 10,000 snow-white horses. The milk from the mares was made into *airag*, the traditional Mongol drink. This *airag* was served only to the Khan's family and the family of his bravest general. Special trainers cared for his 200 hawks.

When Kublai Khan wanted to hunt, he called for his hunters and set out on horseback

had been a great warrior and his mother a powerful leader of the Mongol people. He had four wives of the first rank. His favorite wife, Chabi, was also his close friend and advisor. The eldest son of any of these wives could be his heir, for each wife held the title of Empress. His wives had given him 12 sons, several of whom had been appointed as rulers of China's provinces. The many sons the Khan had fathered with concubines (secondary wives) became soldiers.

Each of the Khan's wives had hundreds of servants. His household numbered thousands. At banquets, his wives and children filled several tables. Nobles, court astrologers, and visitors were placed at other tables. Servants scurried to keep plates and glasses full while the guests laughed at the antics of tumblers

Kublai Khan

Tribute bearers

for the forests. Horsemen shared their saddles with trained leopards and lynxes. When they spotted a deer, the powerful cats were set loose and chased their prey with "savage eagerness and speed," much to the Khan's delight.

The hawks waited their turn on the wrists of their trainers, their eyes alert and beaks open. Trained to hunt small mammals and other birds, they flew off on command, swooped down on their prey, and returned with the kill.

Soon after Marco's arrival, there was a huge celebration at Shang-tu in honor of Kublai Khan's birthday. The Khan appeared in robes made entirely of gold thread, and all of his attendants dressed in silver. Thousands of people arrived from distant provinces. Some brought gifts of precious stones and pearls,

others brought beautiful white horses as an offering for their supreme ruler. Poems were recited in his honor. "Ten thousand years! Ten thousand years!" his subjects shouted, meaning they wished the Khan long life and good health.

Not all of his subjects wished the Emperor a long life. He was the foreign leader of a conquered land, and, though he adopted Chinese ways and customs, many Chinese people still thought of him as a barbarian and resented his rule. Kublai Khan had only lately overpowered the last of the provinces of China that had held out against his grandfather's armies.

The Khan's rule reached across thousands of miles. The huge country required many governors. The Khan placed his most trusted men, his sons and fellow Mongols, to rule over the various provinces of his empire. At court, imperial astrologers, Buddhist monks, and Chinese scholars served as his advisors. Chinese emperors before and after the Khan's rule had also depended on scholars to help them rule. These scholars, called mandarins, studied for years to pass rigorous civil service examinations in order to get the desired positions as advisers in the royal palace. Their knowledge of ancient texts and ways was valuable. Kublai Khan suspended the examinations, but he did keep a staff of Chinese advisers near him.

His government collected tribute from all of its subjects. Peasants sent food from faraway provinces. Artisans were required to devote one day of their week to making clothing and other goods for their emperor. The Khan demanded the finest goods for his court. Providing these extravagant luxuries took its toll on the common people of the land.

The Emperor did not force his subjects to adapt to Mongol traditions, however. He allowed people to practice their own religions and customs. He questioned Marco about Christian beliefs, and he protected those in his empire who practiced Islam. He observed Chinese Confucian rituals and also respected the two other major religions of China, Buddhism and Taoism. Eventually, the Khan became a Buddhist.

The Three Teachings

The traditional Chinese beliefs of Buddhism, Confucianism, and Taoism were together called the Three Teachings. The Buddha's teachings spread throughout China in the first century, 500 years after his death. Confucius and the teacher of Taoism, Lao-tzu, were born around the same time as the Buddha, in the sixth century B.C. Their teachings also shaped Chinese culture and thought.

Confucius was a wandering scholar who lived in a time of war, chaos, and crime. He thought about how to make his world a better place, then taught his disciples about order and harmony. He believed that if everyone behaved in the correct way for their position in the family and in society, then all would be well. He created codes of behavior for every circumstance—rules for how children should behave toward parents, how wives and husbands should treat each other, and how rulers should govern their people. (Confucius was such a stickler for rules that it's said he wouldn't even eat meat unless it was cut into perfect squares!)

Confucius taught that the highest virtues were those of kindness, right behavior, trustworthiness, and respect. His way fit in with the ancient Chinese tradition of ancestor worship. Respect for one's ancestors, and behaving in a way that would do them honor, was considered to be a person's greatest duty.

The Three Teachings (painting of Buddha, Confucius, and Lao-tzu)

According to legend, the wise man Lao-tzu lived for a long time in a Chinese province. One day, he decided to leave. On the back of his water buffalo, he headed out of the gates of his city. As he left, a guard said to him, "Since you are leaving, Lao-tzu, could you write a book to teach me the art of living?" Lao-tzu wrote the book and gave it to him, then departed. The book was called *Tao Te Ching*, the "Book of the Way."

Like Confucius, Lao-tzu was concerned with harmony. But Lao-tzu's teachings focused more on harmony with nature and the universe than within society. These teachings—Taoism—encourage *wu-wei*, or staying in harmony with the flow of things. People are considered to be just one part of the vast universe and can best achieve peace by living simply and accepting change as the natural order of things. "True mastery," said Lao-tzu, "can be gained by letting things go their own way."

Related to Lao-tzu's teachings were the Chinese concepts of yin and yang. These were considered the two great forces in life. Yin stood for darkness, cold, the female, the earth. Yang stood for light, heat, the male, and sky. In Chinese philosophy and art, it was considered important to keep balance and harmony between these two forces.

✖ ✖ ✖

Even though Kublai Khan practiced Chinese traditions, he was still a Mongol. He enjoyed his *airag* and celebrated Mongol holidays. When one of his wives was about to give birth, she moved out of the palace and into a *ger* so the baby would be born in a Mongol home. The Khan even had seeds from the grasses of his homeland planted in the courtyard of the Imperial Palace as a reminder of the grasslands of the Mongolian steppes.

The Imperial Palace, where the Khan spent his winters, was enclosed within four walls, each eight miles long. Marco entered through a gate, accompanied by the royal escort. Their entrance was announced with a clash of drums and cymbals. Within the wall were meadows and trees. Deer lifted their heads to watch the noisy procession. They crossed a mile-long space to a gate in a second wall, topped with parapets and heavily guarded. Within this enclosure stood the many buildings housing the Emperor, his family, and his attendants.

The palace (located near what is now the city of Beijing) was like nothing Marco had ever seen before. He gazed at the bright yellow roofs and the marble staircases. He was awed by the long hallways decorated with marvelous carved

A Qigong Exercise

In the ancient art of qigong (pronounced "chee gung"), yin and yang are in perfect harmony and balance. People who practice it develop their "qi" (energy) through exercises ("gong," meaning skill or practice). Qigong is more than 2,000 years old and is the basis for martial arts such as kung fu.

People all over China practice qigong. They wear comfortable clothes and find a peaceful place (like a park) to find harmony for their bodies and spirits. This exercise, called Cleansing Water, is one of the first exercises they perform.

What you need

A quiet place

Comfortable clothes

1 As you perform this exercise, keep your body relaxed and your mind empty of thoughts. (This can be hard to do—one way is to concentrate on your breathing.) Do the exercise very slowly and easily.

2 Stand with your feet apart (about as far apart as your shoulders) and pointing straight forward. Bend your knees slightly. Hold your back straight and look straight ahead of you. Breathe naturally. Hold your arms at your sides, palms facing forward.

3 Slowly bring your arms up, with palms pointing upward. Imagine, as you do this, that you are scooping up a vast amount of water with your hands. Keep your arms straight, then as you move them up past your shoulders, start to bend your elbows and bring your palms together. Make a half-circle with each arm until your fingertips meet and your palms face the top of your head.

4 Imagine now that you have filled your body with the water. Slowly begin to push it down with your hands—past the top of your head, past your face, and throat. When you push past your eyes, close them. When you inhale, stop your hands. As you exhale, slowly push your hands down again. Keep pushing down on the imaginary water—past your throat, your chest, your stomach, your hips. When your hands are down by your thighs, imagine the water flowing the rest of the way down your legs, past your knees and calves, and down to the very bottoms of your feet.

5 Repeat this exercise 3 times.

dragons, warriors, and birds. Each room seemed to him more beautiful than the last. A whole community was contained within the palace walls, from stables and blacksmith shops to treasuries and harems, where the Emperor's wives and concubines brought up his many children.

The Emperor even had his own personal mountain—the Green Mount. He had his workers raise a large hill, 100 feet high and a mile around, and whenever he saw a new or unusual tree, Kublai Khan had it pulled up by elephants and replanted on this artificial mountain near his palace.

Near the palace was a vast city. It held fine houses with lovely green courtyards and merchants' shops bursting with clothing, food, and goods of every kind. The wide streets of this city were a marvel to Marco, who was used to the twisting, narrow lanes of Italian towns. Each street was as straight as a ruler, so that Marco could see from one gate of the city to the gate at the other end. With its markets and parks laid out in squares, the city seemed to Marco like a giant's chessboard. This design reflected the Chinese belief that the world was a square. The roofs of the houses were not straight but curved, for it was also believed that evil spirits could only travel in straight lines— the curved roofs would stop them from entering the homes!

A T'ang palace

Fun with Feng Shui

*When the Emperor ordered his palace built in a certain place, his advisers objected very loudly! "Bad luck! Bad luck!"
they cried, "If you build it there, a rebellion will occur!" They insisted he change his plans. They were experts in feng
shui (pronounced "fung shway"), the Chinese art of creating a harmonious environment.*

*Have you ever noticed that some places make you feel comfortable right away, while others have "bad vibes"?
Feng shui teaches that everything in your environment has qi (an energy field) that affects your mental and physical
energy. Feng shui experts design buildings and rooms with balanced energy so people feel their best inside them.
Create a do-it-yourself feng shui plan for your room.*

What you need

Pencil and paper

Ruler

Assortment of qi-producing objects,
such as mirrors, wind chimes, bells,
plants, anything red, crystals,
pictures and mementos that make you
feel good

South

Wealth	Fame	Relationships
Family		Creativity & Imagination
Knowledge	Career	Travel & Hobbies

East — West

North

Draw a picture of your room and divide it into nine squares. Label the squares like the chart on page 50. As you can see, the squares represent different areas of your life. According to feng shui, you can create good energy in the squares most important to you by rearranging your room.

Now it's time to inspect your room's qi!

Can't get in the door? A bad sign. Clutter's a real drag. If you've got too much stuff in the way, good energy can't make its way in. Clear a path.

Place your bed in a corner opposite the door for a good night's sleep. Feng shui don'ts—the foot of the bed should not be pointing at the door, mirrors should not face the bed, electronics (televisions and computers) should be far away, and junk should not be stored beneath the bed (it stops the flow of qi). If the only place for your bed is directly in the path of the door, consider placing a folding screen between it and the door.

Place your desk in the Knowledge square and see if your grades improve. According to feng shui, your desk should face the door so you can meet incoming energy head-on. If it's not possible to face the door, hang a mirror over your desk.

Need a creative kick start? Get rid of the dirty socks in your Creativity square and do your painting/writing/music playing there.

Keep a green, growing plant in the Family square for healthy relations with parents and siblings. Water in your Career square might help things flow in this area of your life (how about a goldfish bowl or a rock fountain?). Hang pictures of your best friends in the Relationships corner. Fire (associated with the lucky color red) in the Fame square will light up your chances of celebrity—place red candles (or anything red) in this spot.

Other feng shui tips? Wind chimes and bells revive energy in lifeless corners of a room. Place a crystal near the phone and see if it rings more often. Make sure the lighting in your room is good (darkness is bad qi). Use color to change your luck: green is nourishing and peaceful; yellow is the color of long life. The color red brings good luck, and a red door especially invites it in.

The city around the Khan's palace was crowded and noisy. Merchants bargained in loud voices, street-corner astrologers sold fortunes, and foot messengers wearing bells ran down the streets scattering everyone who got in their way. Dusty traders from faraway places arrived with horses and camels loaded with goods. The Khan encouraged foreign traders to come to his realm. Once within its borders, they had to trade their gold and silver for paper banknotes stamped with the Khan's seal. They could only use these notes to buy goods. Marco thought this was the most amazing idea. Paper money was unheard of in Europe and would not be used there for hundreds of years to come.

Another astonishing custom—people bathed every day! (Where Marco came from, baths were taken very rarely, and only as a cure for gout or rheumatism.) Their baths were heated by a "sort of black stone which they dig out of the mountains which burns better than wood." The black stone was coal, a fuel that was new and quite marvelous to Marco.

At night, the citizens were commanded to go inside their homes and the traders to the inns. After loud bells rang the curfew, no one was allowed on the streets. The curfew was a way to prevent people from gathering. The Khan was anxious to prevent a rebellion against his government. In the thousands of years of Chinese history, many uprisings had occurred.

Who Was First? China!

Paper money was new to Marco Polo. Here are some other Chinese "firsts":

➤ Paper (1,200 years before Europe)

➤ Magnetic compass (600 years before Europe)

➤ Smallpox vaccination (700 years before vaccines were used by westerners)

➤ Chain suspension bridges (1,000 years before Europe)

➤ Gunpowder, discovered accidentally when a Tang Emperor ordered scholars to create a potion for long life

➤ Seismograph (created in A.D. 132. It had eight golden balls balanced in the mouths of eight golden dragons. At the slightest tremor, the balls would drop into the mouths of golden toads sitting beneath them.)

➤ Porcelain (invented around A.D. 900. When Europeans started making it in the 18th century, they called it "china.")

The Chinese were also the first to invent the clock, wheelbarrow, umbrella, fishing reels, cast iron, steel, paddlewheel boats, and noodles—among so many other things! They discovered the principles of photography and guessed that the Earth was round 100 years before Copernicus did. The Chinese were the first to dig for oil, the first to drink tea, and the first to fly kites (2,000 years before anyone in Europe had the idea).

Tea

Tea has been China's most popular drink for 1,000 years! Legend has it that Bodhidharma (the monk who brought Buddhism to China) was having difficulty staying awake during meditation. He cut off his eyelids so he wouldn't fall asleep. They fell to the ground like leaves and the first tea bush grew in the spot where they fell. Monks today still drink tea to stay awake during meditation.

China's Dynasties

The story of the country's earliest recorded era, the Reign of the Five Emperors, is a legendary tale of wise rulers who made up ceremonies and rules for living. According to legend, the last of these emperors founded the Xia Dynasty between 3000 and 2000 B.C. Woven silk as well as pottery and bronze vessels have been found dating back to this era.

Neighboring clans went to war against the Xia Dynasty and established the Shang Dynasty, which lasted over 400 years. During this time, a system of writing developed. The high priests of the Shang family predicted events by reading the patterns of animal bones, but no one knows if they foretold the invasion of a tribe that would dethrone their rulers. This tribe was the Zhou Dynasty, and their reign lasted for 700 years. Zhou warriors wore layers of armor and fought with the crossbow (inventions that would not be used in Europe for many hundreds of years). During this era, peasants tilled their fields with iron plows and Confucius taught his disciples. Nobles, priests, and scholars served their ruler, who was called the Son of Heaven.

Over time, the strength of the Zhou waned, the dynasty broke down, and the country separated into seven warring states. The Qin Emperor, Shihuangdi, conquered and united them and set his subjects to work on the Great Wall.

The Qin Dynasty didn't last long. The peasant who led the revolt against the Qin became the first emperor of the Han Dynasty. During this reign, paper was invented in China, acupuncture was practiced, and trade routes opened to countries to the west. Millions of Chinese began drinking tea. A class of scholars

A Modern Version of an Ancient Art—Making Paper

Early Chinese scholars carved their writings on animal bones. Later, they painted characters on silk or strips of bamboo. One day, someone mixed up a potion of wood pulp, fibers, and water to create paper. Try it yourself!

Adult supervision required

What you need

Scissors

3 pieces of recycled white paper (this will make
   1 piece of handmade paper)

Mixing bowl

Hot tap water

2 pieces of window screen, each 9 inches by
   13 inches

1 jelly roll pan, 10 inches by 15 inches by
   1/2 inch deep

Old towel

Spoon

Blender or food processor

Sponge

4 paper towels

Cutting board

1 Using scissors, cut the recycled paper into 1-inch squares and place them in the mixing bowl. Cover with hot water and let soak for 1 hour. Meanwhile, set one of the screens inside the pan, and spread the towel out on a waterproof table.

2 After an hour, spoon one-fourth of the mushy paper mixture into the blender or food processor. Pour in enough water to cover the paper. Put the lid on the blender and blend until the paper has turned into pulp. Spoon it onto the screen in the pan, then blend another batch. Repeat until all of the paper pulp is used up.

3 When all of the pulp is on the screen, spread it out by patting it gently with your hand. Smooth it out until it is a thin sheet, making sure that the pulp is spread evenly and there are no holes.

4 Carefully lift up the screen and place it on the towel. Put the other screen on top of the pulp. Dampen the sponge and press it down firmly on the top screen. The sponge will soak up some of the water from the paper pulp. Wring it out in the sink and press it down on another spot. Continue doing this until you have pressed the entire surface.

5 Lift the top screen off the pulp. Spread the paper towels over it, then lay the cutting board on top of the paper towels. Press down hard on the cutting board. Remove the cutting board and gently lift off the towels.

6 Gently peel the paper off the screen and set it down someplace where it can dry overnight. When it has completely dried, use it for painting or to write a very special message or poem.

(the mandarins) emerged. They became powerful advisers to the emperors.

After 400 years, the Han dynasty also broke down, and China entered the Age of Disunity. Buddhism spread throughout the land as Buddhist monks traveled along the Silk Road. The Sui Dynasty came to power, but only briefly. The new emperor ordered a great canal built to connect the Yellow River to the Yangtze River. He celebrated the achievement by sailing downriver on his magnificent imperial barge. But his empire was corrupt, and a peasant revolt put a new dynasty in place.

But Did He Read Them All?

One of the Tang Emperors was a real bookworm—he had 40,000 texts on his Imperial bookshelves! He was able to collect all of these books because of the invention of block printing in the ninth century. The world's oldest printed book, *The Diamond Sutra*, dates from this time.

The Dynasties and Republics of China

Xia Dynasty: between 3000 and
2000 B.C.—1557 B.C.

Shang Dynasty: 1557—1122 B.C.

Zhou Dynasty: 1122—481 B.C.

Warring States: 481—221 B.C.

Qin (Ch'in) Dynasty: 221—206 B.C.

Han Dynasty: 202 B.C.—A.D. 221

Age of Disunity: 221—589

Sui Dynasty: 589—618

Tang Dynasty: 618—907

Five Dynasties: 907—960

Song Dynasty: 960—1280

Yuan (Mongol) Dynasty: 1280—1368

Ming Dynasty: 1368—1644

Qing (Manchu) Dynasty: 1644—1911

Republic of China: 1911—1949

People's Republic of China:
1949—present

This family, the Tang Dynasty, placed a female ruler on the throne. Empress Wu, a Buddhist, brought peace and prosperity to her realm, but her descendants did not follow in her footsteps. Another Tang ruler destroyed the Buddhist monasteries. The people revolted once again.

The country split up during the next period (called the Era of the Five Dynasties) until a strong warlord came to power and established himself as ruler of the Song Dynasty. Under Song rule, China was prosperous and its people thriving. It was then, at the end of the 13th century, that the Mongols invaded and came to power. Their period of rule was called the Yuan Dynasty.

Like the emperors before him, Kublai Khan was thought to be the Son of Heaven. His symbol was the dragon, the ruler of water. If the emperor ruled well, abundant rain would fall on his kingdom. The crops and his people would thrive. Kublai Khan performed all the long-established rituals of Chinese tradition, but only time would tell if the people would accept him.

In the Khan's Court

The Polos were given apartments in the winter palace. They were only three more mouths to feed in the huge community. Every day, royal

Gong Xi Fa Cai! (Happy New Year!)

The New Year is the most important holiday in China and is celebrated loudly and happily with fireworks and food. It occurs on a different day in January or February every year, based on the date of the first moon. People clean their houses and pay off old debts, then gather at the homes of their oldest relatives to stay up late and welcome the new year.

One New Year's belief is that a household god, the stove god, will go to heaven on this day to report on the family. Just in case he intends to report a bad thing (or two!), the family bribes him with candy or sticky rice, so that his mouth will be too full to talk.

People eat special cakes and dumplings for good luck and long noodles for long life. Since red is a lucky color, they eat apples, oranges, and tangerines and dress in red clothes. They write poems and lucky sayings on red paper and place them in different parts of the house. ("Always full" is written on red paper and stuck on the rice jar.) Parents give children little red envelopes full of money.

Children are encouraged to stay up as late as possible. Besides, who could sleep at midnight, when all the fireworks go off? The Chinese tradition of shooting fireworks at midnight started with villagers who hoped that the loud noises would scare an evil dragon spirit away.

In the morning, children bring their parents a cup of tea and wish them long life and good health. The first words people say to each other should be lucky, so that good luck will be with them the whole year.

hunters and their mastiff dogs took to the fields and forests to hunt. Many boars, pheasants, and deer were hunted and cooked for the Emperor's table. Thousands of hungry guests needed to be fed.

One day, a very special holiday was celebrated—the first day of the Mongol New Year. Marco called it the White Feast, for the Emperor and all of his subjects wore white on this day. The Khan sat on his throne with his tame lion at his feet. His subjects approached, kowtowed four times, and presented him with rich and wonderful gifts. The Khan's lucky number must have been nine, for he received nine times nine of everything! Many of his subjects brought him 81 perfect white horses for his stables and 81 bolts of fine white silk. Gold, silver, rubies, and pearls piled up near his throne. The highlight of the day was a parade of 5,000 elephants, each carrying a huge chest loaded with gifts. After the parade, the Khan's wives and children, soldiers, advisers, and astrologers all sat down to a great feast.

Acrobats, magicians, and musicians performed while the guests feasted. The Khan laughed at their antics and called for more. Kublai Khan was especially pleased by the actors who put on a play for his guests. The actors sang and danced, using traditional movements that had come down through the

Make a Dragon Mask

The dragon is the symbol of emperors and the luckiest sign of the Chinese zodiac. Wear this mask or hang it on your wall.

What you need

1 sheet each of green, orange, black, and red construction paper, 9 inches by 12 inches

Ruler

Pencil

Scissors

Markers

White glue

Buttons, glitter, and stars (optional)

Lengths of yellow and red ribbon, each 12 inches long

Stapler

1/2-inch wide elastic, 12 inches long

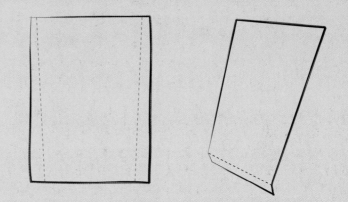

1 Fold the long sides of the green paper along a line that is 1 inch at the bottom and tapers to 1/2 inch at the top. Measure 2 inches from the top and bottom edges and fold down.

2 Pencil in two small triangles near the center of the bottom fold, about 1 inch apart. Cut them out on the fold to make diamond-shaped nostrils. To make your dragon breathe fire, cut 2 pieces of orange construction paper to 1/2 inch by 6 inches. Then cut each of these into 4 very thin strips, leaving a 1/2-inch margin at one end. Insert this end into each nostril and glue to the back of the mask.

3 Draw evil dragon eyes a little above the midpoint of the mask and cut them out. Outline the eyes with a black marker, then outline the black with a red marker. Cut out long, pointed eyebrows from black construction paper and glue them above the eyes. Cut 2 long, curved whiskers from the black paper and glue them below the nostrils.

4 To make a tongue, glue a strip of red construction paper 5 inches long by 1 inch wide to the back of the mask so that it protrudes out from the bottom. Cut a narrow triangle out of its end so that it is forked.

5 Use your markers to draw patterns on the mask. Glue on buttons, glitter, or stars, or draw your Chinese name (see Web Sites to Explore, page 135) on the dragon's forehead. Cut the yellow and red ribbons into thin strips and glue on to the top of the dragon's head.

6 Staple the elastic to the mask on each side at about eye level.

ages. The drama was heightened by their magnificent costumes and masks. Red-faced characters in helmets adorned with feathers were courageous heroes; a blue mask and a colorfully embroidered silk robe adorned the actor playing a sinister mandarin.

In the spring, the Khan's household moved once again to the palace at Shang-tu. Accompanied by his bodyguard of 12,000 horsemen, Kublai Khan traveled in a wide litter carried on the backs of four elephants. He lay across a couch covered with tiger skin; a gold canopy protected him from the sun. His favorite hawk was on his arm, and when his guards told him of game ahead, the Khan freed the bird to hunt. He laughed fiercely when it brought back its prey.

Marco had become a favorite of the Mongol ruler. He was bright and amusing, and his tales of faraway places pleased Kublai Khan. As a newcomer to the court, Marco was innocent of the many palace intrigues. The Khan trusted him. Marco had also mastered four languages since leaving his home in Venice, and this made him very useful to the ruler. Kublai Khan decided to make Marco his emissary (the Khan's representative) and send him on missions to different parts of his kingdom. Marco could observe the people, their customs, and their way of life and report back to their ruler.

ACTIVITY

Stage an Opera—Chinese-Style

Traditional Chinese opera flourished during the reign of Kublai Khan and is still performed today. This type of opera combines singing, dancing, acting, and acrobatics. The actors perform on a stage with very few props. Their movements and songs are accompanied by gongs, cymbals, and delicate stringed instruments. One of the most popular Chinese operas is the fifth-century story of Mulan, a young girl who disguised herself as a boy and became a warrior. Find a story you like and turn it into a Chinese opera.

What you need

A plot

Actors

Costumes (*Collect robes, scarves, and anything that catches your fancy from closets around the house. Use the dragon mask from page 58 for one character. A lovely Chinese maiden could hide behind a fan made of folded paper. Make swords from cardboard and cover the blades with aluminum foil. Use a scarf to make a turban.*)

Makeup (*eyebrow pencil, lipstick, and face paint—for white, use plain cold cream. To make colored face paint, mix 1 tablespoon cornstarch with ½ teaspoon water, 1 tablespoon cold cream, and 8 drops food coloring.*)

Simple props (*a stick, for example, can serve as a staff, a horse, or an oar*)

Musical instruments (*pot-lid cymbals, coffee-can drums*)

An audience

One of the special things about Chinese opera is that it doesn't use complicated backdrops and props. The actors and their costumes are the focus of the play. In Chinese opera, the audience helps by imagining the extras. For example, if you sit on the stage pretending to row, the audience is supposed to guess that you are in a boat. Water can be represented by someone waving a blue scarf close to the floor. One actor carrying a flag will stand for an entire army. You will use exaggerated body movements to show that you are riding a horse, crossing a stream, drinking tea, or walking up a flight of stairs, instead of actually doing these things.

Pick a story to act out. You might like the story of Mulan. This Chinese girl ran away from home disguised as a boy, and learned how to ride a horse and fight like a warrior. She helped save her kingdom from barbarian invasion and won the thanks of everyone, from the peasants to the emperor. Or the Chinese story of the villagers who scared off a marauding dragon with surprise fireworks could make a good play. Or act out the story of

Marco Polo, a clever boy who traveled by horse and camel over mountains and deserts to the magnificent court of Kublai Khan. Along the way he met turbaned bandits, modest monks, Mongols, and mandarins. He saw the great kingdom of Cathay (China) and returned home after a long sea voyage. Write out the story and give copies to all of the actors.

Of course, you'll want to rehearse. The chosen director should tell the actors when and where they should enter and exit the stage and how best to act out their parts. Assign some friends the task of accompanying the actors with sounds. At dramatic moments of the story, have them clash the cymbals. Bang drums while armies march. Remember that Chinese opera includes singing and acrobatics. Make up songs for your characters to sing. At the height of a battle actors could tumble, perform handsprings, and fall beneath enemy swords.

Have a dress rehearsal with costumes and masks. At the real performance, start by explaining to the audience the special things about Chinese opera. Now you're ready to put on your play. Don't forget to kowtow when your audience applauds.

Chinese village

4 The Eyes and Ears of the Khan

For the next 17 years, Marco explored the far-flung provinces of the Khan's conquered empire. He went to places that would not be seen by another European for centuries to come. He traveled through a land that had given birth to one of the world's most ancient civilizations, a land with traditions going back for thousands of years.

His travels took him throughout China, north to the Mongol city of Karakorum, and south to Burma (called Myanmar today), India, and Tibet. He sailed the South China Sea and the Indian Ocean and explored the islands of Java and Sri Lanka. Wherever he went, his most important task was to keep his eyes and ears open. Marco was careful to learn everything he could about the cities and provinces he visited, for he knew that Kublai Khan would want to hear every detail during Marco's return visits to the Emperor's court.

Marco set off on his first mission, excited to be traveling again. He journeyed by horse, stopping at post houses, which were spaced at regular intervals along the roads. These post houses were part of the Khan's imperial mes-senger service, called the Yam. At each post house, horses were kept for the Khan's couriers. The couriers wore bells so they could be heard approaching from far away. By the time they arrived at the post house, a horse was already saddled and waiting for them. They leaped onto the new mount and continued on their journey. In this way, the couriers could travel 300 miles a day and deliver messages quickly to cities all over China.

Travel was pleasant through the green countryside. The tree-lined roads were shady and cool. Marco saw vineyards and orchards of mulberry trees, the leaves of which were used to feed the precious silkworms. He saw fields of ginger, bamboo cane, wheat, and rice. Peasants tilled the fields surrounding their small villages,

Chinese landscape

Still Growing

We know the Tibetan mountain Chomolungma as Mount Everest. At 29,035 feet above sea level, it is the highest mountain in the world. It is part of the Himalayan mountain range, which was formed millions of years ago when free-floating India crashed into the continent of Asia. India is still pushing up against the continent. Because of this, the Himalayas are still growing—at a rate of two inches a year.

making crops to sell in the markets of the bustling cities.

The cities! Marco was stunned to find, in one province after another, large and prosperous cities that made the cities of Europe look like villages. Transportation and communication systems were efficient and wide-reaching. Goods traveled by barge along canals and by wagon along the wide roads.

On this and all of his journeys, Marco rode long miles and traveled for months at a time. He crossed the wide, rushing Yellow River (the Huang He). In earlier times, a young woman had been thrown into the river every year as a

sacrifice to the river god. He crossed the Yangtze River (the Jian); at 3,400 miles long, the Yangtze is the longest river in Asia and third longest in the world. It was so wide that Marco thought it was the sea! He climbed a high mountain range and came to a wild region that had once been inhabited but was now empty of people. Its towns were in ruins, victims of Mongol attacks. Tigers, bears, and other wild animals roamed the streets.

Tibet

After weeks of travel south from the Khan's palace, Marco reached the border of Tibet (once an independent country, now it is a province of China). In this country of grasslands, forests, and steep, snow-covered mountains, the people wore thick furs against the frigid air. Men hunted with dogs and falcons and plowed small fields in mountain valleys with the help of their yaks. The women ground up the barley harvested from the fields and used it to make *tsampa* (barley cakes), which the families ate at home with cups of buttered tea.

In some of the homes, a man had more than one wife. More often, one woman was married to two or more brothers. When babies were born, their parents smudged their faces with soot (to hide them from demons). When they were older, the children helped their parents by fetching water and gathering yak dung to use as fuel. Marriage ceremonies were simple, and the young bride showed her new adult status by donning a colorful apron. After death, people were given a sky burial. Their bodies were taken to a high rocky platform and fed to sacred vultures so their souls could be freed.

According to Tibetan legend, long ago their land was low and forested and almost entirely covered by the ocean. One day, five dragons emerged from the water, creating huge tidal waves and burning the forests with fiery breaths. The forest birds flew wildly against the hot winds and the animals ran in terror. Just as the dragons were about to destroy everything, five good spirits appeared. They commanded the sea to roll back and the dragons to withdraw again under its waters. When the waves withdrew they left behind a rich and fertile land. The spirits then turned into five mountains. Then, according to the legend, the Tibetan people made their appearance, born to a marriage between a monkey and a rock-demon.

From the distant time of the Seven Heavenly Kings (who climbed to the heavens on sky-cords) to the seventh century, the people of Tibet farmed and traded and lived as neighboring tribes. They were unified under Songtsen Gampo, who built the Potala Palace,

Yak

married two foreign queens, and began a powerful dynasty. Both of his wives were Buddhists, and Songtsen Gampo adopted this religion. He ordered the construction of Buddhist temples across the land. Soon thousands of pilgrims and monks (called lamas) bowed and prayed to golden likenesses of the Buddha. Yak-butter lamps sputtered in the dark temples, while outside colorful flags waved in the wind.

Marco thought the Tibetans were magicians. "They cause tempests to arise, accompanied with flashes of lightning and thunder-

Simhavaktra Dakini

bolts," he said. Back at the Khan's palace, Tibetan magicians were ordered to stand on the roof and perform spells to keep bad weather from disrupting the royal schedule. The Khan converted to the Tibetan form of Buddhism (sometimes called Lamaism), which combined Buddhist beliefs with an ancient Tibetan religion called Bon. Magic and spirits were an important part of Bon beliefs.

The Dalai Lama

When the 13th Dalai Lama died in 1935, his regent (the monk who ruled in his place) had a vision of a house with a turquoise roof. He knew this would be the place where the Dalai Lama would be reborn. Groups of monks traveled throughout the country looking for the house with the turquoise roof. Two years later, one group found it. The head monk disguised himself as a servant, put on an old set of beads that had belonged to the Dalai Lama, and knocked on the door.

The two-year-old boy who answered the door demanded the beads, saying they belonged to him. He recognized and named the head monk, even though he was disguised as a servant, and named the others as well. They tested the boy further by placing different objects before him. Without fail, he chose only those that had belonged to him in his previous life. After many trials, the youngster was pronounced the 14th Dalai Lama. He is the Dalai Lama living today.

Tibetan message boards

At the time of Marco's visit, Tibet was ruled by a council of 20 high lamas under Mongol control. Not long after this time, a great monk appeared. The Mongols gave him his name, Dalai Lama, which means "ocean of wisdom." The Tibetans believed that this monk had reached the highest spiritual stage (called Nirvana) but had chosen to stay in the cycle of life in order to help others. When this first Dalai Lama died, he reincarnated and came back again as the second Dalai Lama. In his fifth return, he became Tibet's spiritual and political leader.

Marco's adventures continued. He visited different Chinese provinces, each ruled by sons of the Khan. In one province, the people wore

Make a Mandala

Tibetan monks create intricate mandalas (circular sand paintings in geometric patterns) that symbolize the circle of life. They use these paintings as a focus during meditation. They spend days arranging colored sand into a patterned circle, picking up and placing one grain of sand at a time. When the mandala is finished, they hold a ceremony and sweep their hard work away. Combine art and geometry to make a sand mandala of your own. (Warning: for the last part of this activity, you might want to make sure you're outside.)

What you need

Paper

Pencil

Ruler

At least 4 plastic bottles with tips (like the bottles used on picnics for ketchup and mustard, or clean recycled honey bottles)

Colored sand in 4 or more colors (found at craft stores)

mandalas

1 Traditional mandalas start with outlines of geometric shapes. On your paper, draw the basic design shown here or create one of your own. Proportion and symmetry are important—traditional mandalas are exactly balanced and centered.

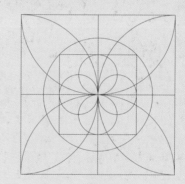

2 Fill each of the bottles with a different color of sand. Fill in one section of the mandala drawing at a time by squeezing the sand out of the bottle onto the drawing. Carefully fill in the remaining sections. When you are done with your drawing take a few moments to admire it. Then sweep it away!

heavy leather armor and carried poison arrows as protection against "huge serpents, ten paces in length, with glaring eyes and jaws wide enough to swallow a man." (This was Marco's first sight of a crocodile.) In another province, the people practiced an unusual custom after the birth of a baby. The woman immediately got out of bed and her husband laid down on it. There he stayed for 40 days. Friends and relatives visited the man to congratulate him on the birth of the child, while the mother cooked and cleaned and nursed the infant!

Myanmar

On another trip, Marco traveled far to the south, over mountains, across a wide plain, and through dense bamboo forests. He saw elephants and rhinoceroses (because of its single horn, he mistook the rhino for the legendary unicorn). Finally he reached Burma (today's Myanmar). Marco described how its king, with an army of trained archers on the backs of huge elephants, faced the Mongol hordes across a large plain. Though outnumbered five to one, the Mongols triumphed in a battle "so great that the clangor of arms and shouts of men ascended to the skies." Like so many others, the native people fell under Mongol rule. They had been in this land for as long as they could

Tigers in Danger

Once found from Siberia to India, and from Iran to Japan, the tiger is now close to extinction. Three of eight subspecies of tigers became extinct in the 1900s. Scientists believe there are only between 3,000 and 6,000 tigers left in the wild today.

The tiger is the biggest member of the cat family, with Siberian tigers weighing nearly 700 pounds. These solitary animals need a lot of territory for hunting. They mark their boundaries with urine and scent glands so other tigers know to stay away. Tigers quietly track their prey (deer, wild boar, and other large mammals), then pounce for the kill. After a successful hunt they gorge—a hungry tiger can eat 40 pounds of meat in one meal!

A mother raises her cubs (usually two, born blind and weighing only three pounds) for two to three years. She teaches them how to hunt and care for themselves.

In many places, the tiger habitat has been destroyed. Poachers kill tigers for their beautiful striped pelts and for the body parts still used in Chinese folk medicines. The governments of India and other southeast Asian countries are making efforts to conserve tiger habitat, and the government of China has agreed to try to stop the use of endangered species in traditional medicines.

Tiger

legs. Farther on, Marco came to a land where people made clothing from the bark of trees. This country was wild and was inhabited by so many tigers that people didn't dare leave their homes except with their large and fierce dogs.

Southern China

In the southeast part of China, Marco found a more populated land. Its many cities and towns were all subject to the Great Khan's rule. It had taken the Mongols many years to conquer these lands.

When the first Mongol invaders swept into China, one of the Chinese Emperor's sons escaped and proclaimed himself the new Emperor of the Song Dynasty. He fled to the south and established his royal capital in a city that Marco called Quinsai (today's Hangzhou). Years later, Kublai Khan sent his best general, Chinsan Bayan ("Old Hundred-Eyes"), to capture the city and the Song Emperor. As the general and his armies marched toward the Song capital, they destroyed towns and burned fields. Just before they reached the capital, the Emperor died, leaving his four-year-old son and the boy's grandmother to face the Mongol army.

The boy emperor and his grandmother surrendered to General Bayan. (Marco said it had

remember. According to legend, their ancestors had followed a golden deer to this place, which they named "wondrous land." It was so beautiful, they stayed forever.

When Marco entered the capital city of this kingdom he was awed at the sight of two pagodas (towers) gleaming in the sun, one covered with silver and the other with gold. They were temples built over the tomb of an ancient king. The Mongols had left them standing, since they considered it a sin to destroy or remove anything built in honor of the dead.

The people of this country were tattooed all over their bodies with figures of birds and beasts. Those with the most tattoos were considered to be the most beautiful. In a neighboring province, men and women wore bracelets of gold and silver on their wrists, arms, and been predicted that the Emperor would only surrender to a hundred-eyed monster. The Mongol general's nickname, Old Hundred-Eyes, fulfilled the prediction.) They were taken to the Khan's palace, where the youngster was treated well. In time, he became a Buddhist monk. His half-brother, who might have carried on the dynasty, escaped but drowned as he tried to flee from the Mongol army. Southern China and the great city of Quinsai were now under Mongol rule.

Quinsai

Marco had never seen anything like Quinsai, the "city of heaven." This magnificent city was the largest and most prosperous city in the entire world at that time. It was 100 miles around, with a million inhabitants.

Quinsai was surrounded by water, with a lake on one side and a great river on the other. Canals entered through gates in the high, white town walls and flowed through the city, reminding Marco of his hometown of Venice. Bridges arched over the canals, allowing tall-masted vessels to pass through the city. Boats of all kinds traveled along the canals. There were barges loaded with rice, small fishing boats bringing the day's catch to the city's mar-

What's in a Name?

The Chinese city that Marco called Quinsai is known today as Hangzhou. Not long ago it was called Hangchow. If you use older maps and books, you'll find that the cities and regions of China have different names from the names we use today. An old book might list China's capital as Peking; we call this city Beijing. In 1958, a new system of translating Chinese words into western languages was adopted. The letter *p* was replaced with *b* (that's how Peking became Beijing), *d* replaced *t*, and many other changes were also made.

kets, and boats carrying fruit, bright flowers, and vegetables. Other boats served as taxis.

The city overflowed its borders. Outside its walls, a jumble of houses and shops spilled over the landscape. On their outskirts, peasants fished, hunted, and tended crops. Whole families worked together, the boys in the fields and boats with their fathers, and the girls weaving fine silk or making fabric from hemp or cotton.

Inside the city's walls, multistoried houses stood side by side, their bright yellow and green roofs nearly touching. The shops of jewelers, calligraphers, hat makers, and book peddlers lined the streets. In other shops, astrologers told fortunes and doctors used herbs and acupuncture needles to restore qi (vital energy) to their patients. Horse-drawn carriages clattered down the streets, with finely dressed ladies peering out from behind their curtains.

Quinsai delighted all the senses. Pear and plum trees flowered and bore fruit. The city's 100 arched bridges were painted in bright colors. Statues of dragons and phoenixes guarded the rooftops of the buildings and stone lions snarled at the gates. Red lanterns hung over doorways. In 10 large markets, goods from all over the land enticed buyers. Pheasants and rabbits hung in stalls. Dried fish, noodles, and rice spilled out from large baskets. The smell of spices, perfumes, and incense hung in the air. Pet crickets sang from their wicker cages. People gathered in the city's gardens to hear storytellers shape tales of ancient heroes and watch acrobats tumble. They laughed and cried at the fortunes of characters in operas.

Others visited the city's gardens to paint—or to meditate on the water lilies, ponds, and rocks in preparation for painting. In Chinese

English words are made up of letters that represent sounds. You can "sound them out." Many Chinese words are represented by characters called pictographs (drawings that look like the things they are supposed to represent, like a tree). Others are ideographs. These are pictographs that, combined together, suggest an abstract idea (for example, the symbols for "ear" and "door" are combined to produce the symbol for "news"; the symbol for "escape" is a combination of the symbols for "mouse" and "hole").

It's easy to learn the English alphabet of 26 letters. How long would it take you to memorize the 6,000 characters that are in common use in Chinese? A really well-educated Chinese person might know as many as 25,000 characters!

Say It in Chinese

Tai chi and *feng shui* are Chinese words we already use (along with chop suey and egg fu yung!). China is so big and has such a huge population that, though everyone understands a common written language, at least eight different spoken languages are used throughout the country. The following words are from Mandarin, the most commonly used Chinese language:

Hello: Nǐ Hǎo *(knee how)*

Goodbye: Dzaì jìan *(zye jen)*

Please: Qǐng *(ching)*

Thank you: Xiè xiè
(shee-yeh shee-yeh)

Yes: Shì *(shy)*

No: Bù *(buh)*

felt complete understanding of that mountain or that cat. When the qi of the artist and the qi of the animal, plant, or mountain became one, then the painting could begin.

Traditional landscape painting was called *shanshui* (meaning "mountains and water"). By placing both mountains and water in their paintings, artists showed harmony and balance. Mountains represented the strength and force of yang. Water represented the serenity of yin. Landscapes were detailed and realistic, made with simple brush strokes, and painted on long, hanging scrolls. If people were placed in the landscapes, they were very tiny figures. This reflected the belief that humans are only a small part of nature.

People of all kinds thronged the streets. Wealthy women, dressed in silks, their hair pinned up with ivory combs, were followed by servants carrying their purchases. Beggars cried out for their attention; thieves quietly tried to pick their pockets.

The wealthy merchant and mandarin families of Quinsai kept many servants. Musicians and tutors taught their children. Gardeners tended perfect miniature gardens, complete with small lakes crossed by exquisite bridges, circular moon gates, and tiny waterfalls. Within the walls of the residences, separate buildings housed the family and the servants. Other

art, it was very important to capture the true essence (the qi) of the landscape or animals the artist painted. The best artists spent time contemplating nature. They meditated on the essence of the mountain or the cat until they

Chinese street scenes

buildings held altars that were visited on special occasions.

Furnishings were sparse. Carefully arranged flowers were placed on low rectangular tables. Wooden beds were hidden discreetly behind painted screens. The wealthy families had furniture painted in black lacquer (red was reserved for the emperor). Landscape scrolls hung on the walls. Spoiled, fat cats slept on low chairs.

The families ate their meals at the low tables, with many courses served in small porcelain dishes. Slurping bird's nest soup with porcelain spoons was considered quite proper! They pushed rice, noodles, and bean curd to their mouths with chopsticks, and they drank their rice wine hot.

The women of wealthy families were encouraged to be timid and delicate; some were even confined to their homes. They wore white makeup, plucked their eyebrows into thin lines, and painted their nails with polish made from pink balsam leaves. Perfume sachets swung from their belts.

Chinese-Style Painting

Favorite subjects for Chinese artists were landscapes, flowers, birds, and other animals. During the Yuan (Mongol) Dynasty, painters chose subjects pleasing to their rulers—such as horses! For this activity, you might want to paint a tree or your cat. Just make sure you get in touch with its qi first.

What you need

Newspaper

Watercolor paper

Bamboo brush (these come in several sizes—you might want to start with a good-quality #3 brush)

Black watercolor paint

Cup of water

1 Start painting by setting aside your paints and brushes! Go outside, find a place in nature, and sit quietly. Take in your surroundings. Look carefully at a tree, notice its rough bark, and watch the way its leaves move in the wind. Think about what it would be like to be that tree—rooted, soaking in sunshine, your toes deep in the earth. Look at a bird and imagine feeling the soft feathers. Watch the way it moves its head and flutters its wings.

2 When you're satisfied that you've reached a deep understanding of your surroundings, you're ready to paint. Lay newspaper out to cover your work surface, then set out the watercolor paper. Plan the composition of your painting. For a vertical painting you will want elements of height—tall trees will bring a forceful yang element to your painting. You can balance this with the yin of a lake or river and the addition of small details (like a sparrow or a tiny human figure).

3 To paint in the Chinese style, use the traditional brush strokes ancient artists developed for calligraphy (the art of writing). For the bone stroke, hold the brush vertically (upright) and don't allow your hand to touch the paper. When you are ready to make a stroke, dip the brush with water and paint, lower it to the paper, paint the intended line or mark in one movement, then lift the brush up again. (It takes practice!) To gradually make a line thicker, touch the tip of the brush against the paper, then gradually press it down

harder as you move along the line (see drawing). Use long, uninterrupted lines for the yin elements and short, choppy strokes (called ax-cut strokes) to show the movement and energy of yang. The waterdrop stroke is made with the side of the brush. Hold the brush nearly sideways, press it against the paper, and lift it up.

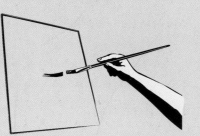

4 Chinese painters finished their paintings by writing a short poem on it. Add a poem that reflects your feelings about your painting.

by Olivia Lenny Hill, age 15

At the time of Marco's visit to China, it was possible to tell someone's class and rank by the clothes they wore. Only a high-ranking mandarin official would dare to wear green! Umbrellas (a Chinese invention) were carried only by princes of the royal family. A merchant could be recognized by his trousers. Servant girls wore bangs and pigtails, and military men sported long mustaches and goatees. Silk was a luxury of the rich; peasants wore clothing made of hemp.

Within each household, several generations of a family lived together. According to Confucian custom, the youngest members of the family showed strict obedience and respect to their elders. They did not answer back when their parents spoke to them and never sat down when an elder was present. But even though they were taught to be polite and very obedient, children were rarely disciplined. Only especially naughty children were told that Big-Eyes Yang (with the terrible, booming voice) or Liu the Barbarian would come to eat them.

Boys from well-to-do families went to school to learn to read and write, use the abacus, and play music. As they grew older, they studied ancient texts and poems in the hopes of passing the examinations to become a mandarin. Some girls also attended school, but most simply learned how to embroider, sing,

Noodles

Many people think that Marco Polo brought noodles back with him from China and introduced Italians to pasta. Not true! Marco did see Chinese people eating noodles and wrote about it in his journal, but the people back home had been eating pasta for some time. Pasta is mentioned in an Italian cookbook from the year 1000 and in a twelfth-century travel book about Sicily. In 1279, before Marco's return, an Italian lawyer listed "a basket of macaroni" among the items owned by his client.

Arabs had been eating dried pasta for years. It was excellent ready-made food for desert travel. The Chinese had been making noodles for centuries—possibly as far back as 1100 B.C. In 300 B.C., a Chinese scholar wrote a poem about noodles!

In China, noodles are sometimes wide, sometimes thin, but they're always long. Long noodles symbolize long life, making them a common dish at birthday celebrations. Chinese noodles are made of wheat or rice or bean paste and served hot or cold, steamed, fried, or boiled. Marco might have seen noodle-makers pulling dough at the market, stretching and twirling it until the strings were long and thin. This was an improvement over the method of Italian cooks at the time, who kneaded pasta dough with their feet!

Chinese Stir-Fry

Stir it up and get wok-y! You might even like vegetables if you make them Chinese-style. This recipe serves 4.

Adult supervision required

What you need

1 cup white rice

Saucepan with lid

2 tablespoons vegetable oil

Wok or frying pan

½ teaspoon chopped ginger

½ teaspoon chopped garlic

½ cup each of four different chopped vegetables (use red, yellow, or orange peppers, snow peas, broccoli, mushrooms, bok choy, or any other favorite vegetable)

Wooden spoon

½ pound tofu, cubed

Soy sauce

Green tea

Serving bowls and cups

Chopsticks

1 Cook the rice in the saucepan according to the directions on the package.

2 Heat the oil over medium-high heat in the wok or frying pan. Add the ginger and garlic and cook, stirring, for 30 seconds. (Be careful of spattering oil.) Add the vegetables and cook, stirring, for 5 minutes. Add the tofu and cook and stir for 1 minute longer. Remove from heat. Add soy sauce to taste.

3 Boil water and make a pot of green tea.

4 Place the rice and vegetables in large bowls. Set them on the table with the pot of tea, serving dishes, tea cups, and chopsticks. Toast the health of your guests with your tea, and dig in!

5 Make sure you fill your guests' teacups whenever they are empty. If they are Chinese, they know that if they don't want any more tea, they should leave some in their cups.

and play musical instruments. Peasant children helped their families. In middle-class households, the boys usually followed their fathers' footsteps and became merchants or craftsmen. Girls became servants, seamstresses, cooks, musicians, or concubines.

When girls turned 15 and boys 20, they were considered adults and ready for marriage. Marriages were arranged by the families. Often the bride and groom had never met! Arrangements were made with the help of astrologers and go-betweens (the go-betweens were women who worked in pairs). The families gave them cards with the prospective bride's and groom's names and birth dates. The go-betweens took the cards to an astrologer to see if the match would be lucky. (No engagement would take place unless the astrologer foresaw a fortunate match.) The families then exchanged information about their ancestors and their property.

If all seemed well, the bride and her family visited the groom's home for the Ceremony of the Cups. The parents exchanged promises over cups of rice wine, and the groom placed two hairpins in his fiance's hair. The groom's family gave gifts of gold and rice wine; the bride's gave cloth, two sticks, and two bowls of goldfish.

On the wedding day (chosen by the astrologer for the best possible luck), the bride and her family marched in a procession to the groom's family home, while people along the street showered her with seeds, beans, and coins. A young girl walked backward in front of the bride, holding a mirror. When the bride stepped into her new family's home, she was taken into a curtained room to await her husband. She was now part of a new family, and rarely—if ever—could she visit her own parents again. Even if her husband died, she stayed with her in-laws to care for them when they grew old.

Emperors and other members of the royal family could take more than one wife. It was not uncommon for concubines to be brought in as members of a wealthy household. They added to the family's honor by bringing more children. It was considered an especially great honor to become a concubine in the Imperial Palace. If no son was born to the Empress, a concubine's son could become emperor.

The birth of a child was awaited with much anticipation, for then the family name could continue. Because a daughter left to become part of her husband's family, it was considered very important to have sons. The son and his future wife would care for his parents in their old age and provide grandchildren.

In middle-class families, one month before a baby was due, its grandparents gave presents

A Fishy Story

Chinese fishermen used an unusual technique to catch fish—they trained birds to do it for them! They tied cords around the long necks of cormorants so they couldn't swallow the fish, then sent them diving underwater to fish. When the fishermen's baskets were full, they slipped the cords off the birds and allowed them to dive again to catch food for themselves.

How to Use Chopsticks

Using chopsticks can be tricky. Place one so that it rests on your third finger and goes between your thumb and first finger. Press against it with your thumb. Hold the other chopstick above it just like you would hold a pencil, using the tip of the thumb and the first and second fingers to move it. The bottom chopstick should remain stationary; the top one does all the moving. Hold them close to the eating end—they'll be easier to control.

When eating rice, it's proper to bring your bowl up to your mouth and "shovel" the rice in with your chopsticks. It's considered rude to leave rice uneaten (an insult to the farmers who grew it). When you're finished eating, place your chopsticks across your empty bowl.

to hasten the birth, enticing it with beautiful clothing and silver platters piled with delicious foods. When the baby was born, its parents wrote down the exact minute and hour of the birth for the astrologers. After the baby turned one month old, it received its first bath (in a silver bowl) and first haircut. Its baby locks were stored in a golden box. The mother then held the baby and kowtowed to each family member in turn. On its first birthday, another special ceremony was held. The baby was set down in the middle of the floor and objects were placed around it—a book, needle and thread, flowers, a jeweler's scale. Whatever object the baby reached out to grab foretold its future occupation.

There were also ceremonies when death came. Each member of the family grieved according to the required custom. They cut their hair and put on coarse clothing. The women wailed and beat their chests. Paper images of horses and servants were burned so that the dead person would be accompanied by them in the next world. Feng shui masters were consulted about the proper burial place. Everyone followed the coffin down the streets, playing musical instruments and singing in honor of their ancestor. When they came home again, they placed a tablet with the name of the person on an ancestral altar. This way, the per-

Make a Paper Lantern

The Lantern Festival is still held in China. People compete to see who can make the most beautiful paper lanterns. They shape them like dragons or horses, or even like an emperor on his throne. Make this lantern in the shape of a fish, or try other shapes.

What you need

6 18-inch paper-wrapped wire floral stems (available at craft stores)

Tape

2 twist ties (from bread bags or garbage bags)

Newspaper

White glue

Brightly colored tissue paper

Scissors

Needle and thread

1 Tape two of the stems together to make one long stem. Bend them into the shape of a fish and tape the tail end. Tape two more stems together and make an identical fish shape. Use the twist ties to tie the two fish shapes together—one at the base of the tails and one at the very front of the fish. Twist tightly and tuck the ends toward the inside of the fish.

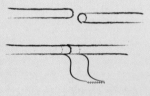

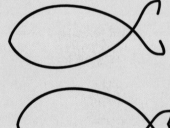

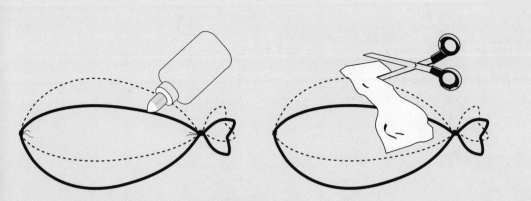

2 Carefully bend the two tails away from each other. Give the fish a three-dimensional body by pulling out on the stems near the middle (see drawing).

3 Spread newspaper out on your workspace. Now you're ready to cover the lantern. Spread glue around the edges of one section of the fish. Gently cover the section with tissue paper and press it carefully against the glued edges. Trim it very carefully with the scissors, cutting as close as you can to the stems. Now cover another section. Continue until the fish is entirely covered.

4 Thread the needle and carefully push it through the paper right where the fish's mouth would be. Remove the needle from the thread. Tape the remaining two stems together, and tie the thread to the remaining stem so your fish looks as if it's hanging from the end of a fishing pole.

son's spirit would continue to reside in the home. On birthdays and during special festivals, they burned incense and candles in front of the tablet.

Chinese Festivals

Many festivals were celebrated throughout the year. Soon after the big New Year holiday, the Feast of Lanterns was held. Lanterns in every color decorated the homes and shops. Women in silk dresses played flutes and stringed instruments. Tightrope walkers balanced precariously over the streets, walking across ropes strung between buildings. Boxing matches and juggling and storytelling contests were held all night long.

The anniversary of Buddha's entry into Nirvana was honored with streamers, flowers, and visits to monasteries. People bought turtles, fish, and birds in the markets and set them free in a ceremony called the "Liberation of Living Creatures."

The Festival of the Dead was celebrated in the spring. For three days beforehand, all fires were put out. People ate cold food or none at all. When the holiday arrived, a palace official kindled a fire by drilling two sticks together. Torches lit from this small flame were brought to homes around the city so people could light their fires again. Everyone decorated their homes with green branches and brought offerings to the graves of their ancestors. They drank new rice wine and danced in the streets. Drummers led crowds to the lake outside the city's walls to watch the Jousting of the Dragon Boats. In this event, six ships decorated with flowers and flags faced each other in pairs. When a giant gong beat the signal, the sailors rowed toward their opponents. Then they picked up long pikes and tried to push each other off the boats. The spectators on shore laughed and applauded wildly when the sailors fell into the water, then they walked home in the dark, happy and tired.

The fifth day of the fifth month was not a festival—it was considered to be a very unlucky day. This day belonged to the scorpion, wasp, centipede, snake, and toad. People wore lucky charms and bought special cakes made in five colors to ward off evil spirits. The seventh day of the seventh month was the Festival of Weaving. On this day, everyone wore new clothes. Girls caught spiders and put them in boxes. They set them free the next morning, after the spiders wove a web for them.

Autumn brought the Moon Festival. An ancient legend told that the moon was devoured every month by a black toad. On this night, people stayed up late and sat on their

Your Chinese Name

Chinese names are different from ours in the western world. They place the family name (our last name) first, and the given name (our first name) last (and often in two parts). Marco Polo might have been Polo Mar-co. If you meet a man named Li Po, address him not as Mr. Po, but as Mr. Li. Chinese names are often references to objects or characteristics, such as "Precious Pearl" or "Worthy Friend." (See Web sites on page 121 to find out your Chinese name.)

roofs, playing music and eating special moon cakes. They watched the moon move across the sky and looked for the black toad.

Even ordinary days in Quinsai seemed special. The city began stirring before sunrise when bells rang at the Buddhist and Taoist monasteries. Those who didn't hear the bells were awakened by monks who walked the city streets banging on drums and calling out the day's weather and news. Merchants opened their stalls and peasants streamed in from the countryside with supplies. Peddlers sold hot water for washing up. At home, people ate breakfasts of fried tripe and steamed pancakes.

Crowds thronged the markets, noodle shops, and tea houses until evening.

As the sun began to set, scholars walked to the city's gardens to play chess or write poetry. Children played in large groups in the streets until their parents called out to them to come home.

Marco returned again and again to Quinsai. He always found it hard to leave, but his duties to the Khan called him back to the Imperial Court.

ACTIVITY

Three Chinese Games

Jug (or "Narrow-Neck")

This game was popular in 13th-century Quinsai. Play this version with one or more friends. Place three containers, each one smaller than the next, in a line (for example, you can use a big bowl, a gallon milk jug with the top cut off, and an empty coffee can). Stand back and take turns trying to make a ping-pong ball bounce once off the floor and into the largest container. Then try to bounce it into the next smaller container. Good luck trying to bounce it into the smallest one!

Stone-Paper-Scissors

You may have played this game, which was invented in China. Two people face each other. Each makes a fist with one hand. Call out "Stone-paper-scissors" and, on the last word, quickly put this hand out in front of you in one of three positions—flat for paper, in a fist for stone, and with two fingers out for scissors. Who wins? Stone beats scissors (by crushing them), scissors beats paper (by cutting it), and paper beats stone (by covering it up). If two players make the same gesture it's a tie!

Eagle and Chicks

This is a rowdy outdoor game for a group of kids to play. One person is the eagle, one a mother hen, and the rest are baby chicks. The chicks line up behind their mother, holding onto each other's waists, with the first chick holding onto Mom's. The eagle tries to catch a chick by getting around the mother to tag one. The mother hen spreads her wings and tries to stay in front of her chicks, facing the eagle no matter where he goes. When the eagle tags a chick, that chick becomes the eagle.

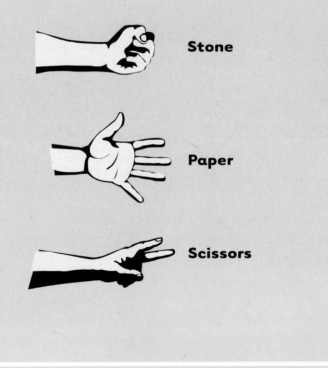

Stone

Paper

Scissors

Moon Cakes

Traditional moon cakes are more like cookies. They are baked with fillings like red bean paste, yams, or nuts. (Later, you'll read how the Chinese people baked moon cakes with secret messages in them!) This recipe makes 18 moon cakes.

Adult supervision required

What you need

2 mixing bowls

Beaters

Spatula

Wax paper

Saucepan

Rolling pin

Round cookie cutter

Cookie sheet

For dough:

½ cup softened butter

1 cup sugar

2 eggs

1 teaspoon vanilla

2½ cups flour

¼ teaspoon baking soda

½ teaspoon salt

For filling:

1 cup ground walnuts

½ cup sugar

1 tablespoon butter

1 tablespoon milk

1 To make the dough, beat the butter, sugar, eggs, and vanilla in one bowl until smooth. In the other bowl, stir together the flour, baking soda, and salt. Add these ingredients to the butter mixture and stir until blended. Remove the dough from the bowl, wrap it in a sheet of wax paper, and put it in the refrigerator for 1 hour.

2 While the dough is chilling, make the filling. Put the ground walnuts in a bowl with the sugar. Place the butter and milk in a pan and heat on low until the butter is melted. Add it to the walnut-sugar mixture and stir.

3 Heat the oven to 400° F. Lightly grease a cookie sheet. Roll out the dough on a floured surface. For each moon cake, cut two round cookies with the cookie cutter. Put one of the rounds on the cookie sheet. Place a teaspoon of the filling in the middle of the round and spread it out a little. Cut a crescent moon shape in the middle of the other round, then place the second round on top of the filling. Press the edges together with your fingertips. Place in the oven and bake for 10 minutes, or until edges are slightly brown.

5 Journeys by Junk

Marco's travels took a new turn when the Khan asked him to visit India and Sri Lanka. Now he traveled by sea, sailing with a fleet of Chinese junks. These were four-masted vessels with raised square decks in the front and back, and 10 pairs of oars, each pulled by four men.

Before setting off on a long journey, the Chinese sailors held a special (and dangerous) ceremony. They strapped a man to a giant kite and lifted it high in the air. If the kite rose and flew, the ship's journey would be a lucky one. If it crashed into the sea, it was a sign of bad luck (it was certainly bad luck for the man strapped to the kite!) and the journey was put off until another time.

With square sails raised and the sailors pulling with all their strength, Marco's fleet of junks set off on their journey. They traveled for long weeks at sea. Sometimes the boats were bumped by curious whales and the sailors rushed to repair the holes made by the giant creatures. At night, Marco stood on the deck, watching the white foam left in his ship's wake and the thousands of unfamiliar stars wheeling overhead.

The fleet stayed far away from the coast of Japan. Three times, Japan had driven back the attacks of Mongol armies. Marco heard stories about its royal palace with roofs of gold and the magical feats of the Japanese warriors. It was said that when the Khan's soldiers attacked, their swords bounced off the necks of the Japanese warriors as if they were made of steel! After two defeats, Kublai Khan sent a 150,000-man army in 4,000 ships against Japan. As the ships approached the shore, the Kamikaze (Divine Wind) began to blow. Giant waves, called tsunamis, engulfed the thousands of ships. The Khan's army drowned at sea.

Marco's ship hugged the coast of China. It stopped just south of Kublai Khan's empire (in today's Vietnam). This country was also free from Mongol rule, but its king sent an annual tribute to the Khan—20 of the largest elephants to be found in his country's forests, along with ships full of sweet-scented wood.

Indonesia

The fleet was nearing the equator. In the seas ahead were thousands of islands (many of which now make up the country of Indonesia). Some were huge countries, and others were as small as a house. Some were alive with smoldering volcanoes. Many were thick with jungle vines, orchids, and banyan trees. Monkeys, pythons, and brightly colored birds lived in their forests. During this journey and a later one, Marco's fleet made stops at several of these islands.

Other ships visited the islands, too. In the ports of Java, Marco saw Chinese and Arab merchants trading for the island's peppers, nutmeg, and cloves. In Sumatra (which Marco called "Java the Lesser"), they traded for spices, dyes, and gold. Here, Marco noted, eight kings ruled eight kingdoms, each with its own language. When unfavorable winds prevented his ship from leaving, he and his sailors built a strong fort to sleep in, with a moat around it for safety.

Long ago, the people of these islands worshiped the sacred spirits in nature around them. In the second century, Indian sea merchants came to trade and shared their religious traditions with the islanders. By the time Marco visited, he noted that most of the people he met had been converted to Islam by Arab traders. All of these different cultures and religions became mixed with Indonesian beliefs. Carved figures of ancient native gods stood side by side with Indian religious figures. Devout Muslims on the islands prayed five times a day.

Java Man

Early Indonesians came to the islands from the Asian mainland 4,000 to 5,000 years ago. That might seem like a long time ago, but long before these migrants arrived, Indonesia was home to some of the earliest human beings. A human species called Homo erectus (not a direct ancestor of our species, Homo sapiens, but a closely related human), lived on the island of Java approximately 1.7 million years ago. The fossil remains of this creature (nicknamed Java Man) were discovered there in 1891. Evidence showed that these early humans stood erect when they walked and used fire and tools.

Sri Lanka

When the winds shifted, Marco's ship traveled west across the Bay of Bengal to the mountainous jungle island of Serendib (later called Ceylon; today it is Sri Lanka). Kublai Khan had sent other ambassadors to this place. He wanted them to obtain a ruby so wondrous that its reputation had reached the Khan thousands of miles away. The ruby belonged to the king of Serendib. It was as thick as a man's arm, and, Marco said, "brilliant beyond description, with the appearance of a glowing fire." Though the Khan offered the "value of a city" for this jewel, the king refused to give it up, for the ruby had belonged to the king's family for many generations.

Marco's mission in Serendib was to obtain another treasure—a begging bowl, thought to have been the Buddha's, that was kept in a shrine at the top of a high, rocky mountain. The king graciously shared the treasure. When couriers returned with this sacred object, all the people of the Khan's imperial city lined the streets to watch the procession carrying the relic to the palace.

ACTIVITY

Batik

Batik is a special way of dying fabrics so that a design appears on both sides. Marco saw people making indigo (blue) dye, but you can use any color for this activity. You <u>must</u> have an adult present for this activity. The hot wax can cause a bad burn and must be used <u>very</u> carefully.

Adult supervision required

What you need

Lots of newspaper

White cotton cloth, 12 inches by 12 inches (recycle an old sheet)

Pencil

4 different colors of crayons

Paraffin (also called "household wax")

Clean, recycled aluminum cans (the 8-ounce size is perfect)

Large pot, filled with one inch of water

Oven mitts

Several paintbrushes

Dry, all-purpose dye (1 ⅛-ounce package) and hot water

Bucket

Old spoon

Paper towels

Iron

1 Spread newspaper over a table for your workspace. Draw your design in pencil on the white cloth (the first time you do this, you might want to start with something simple).

2 Peel the paper off the crayons. Place one crayon and ½ ounce of paraffin in each aluminum can. Put the cans in the large pot with the water and place it on low heat on the stove until the crayon and paraffin is melted. Wearing the oven mitts, take the cans out of the water and place them on your workspace.

3 Paint your design on the white cloth with paintbrushes dipped in the melted colored wax. Leave small lines of white between the colors on your design. (If the colored wax hardens while you work, you might need to melt it again.) Let the wax cool completely on the cloth until it is hard. Then gently crumple the cloth, so that the wax cracks.

4 Have an adult mix a batch of dye with hot water in a bucket (for a piece of cloth 12 inches by 12 inches, a quarter-package of dye will do the trick). *Let the dye cool*, stir your cloth into it, and let it sit for 10 minutes. Have the adult remove your cloth from the bucket, wring it out, and lay it flat on the newspaper to dry.

5 Lay out several sheets of fresh newspaper and place two or three paper towels on top of it. Place your cloth on the paper towels, cover with more paper towels and several sheets of newspaper. Have your adult helper iron it through the paper with a medium iron. They may have to do so several times, until the wax has soaked into the papers and is all gone from the cloth.

6 Your batik artwork is complete. You can hang this piece of art either way, for the design appears on both sides of the cloth.

India

From Serendib it was only a short distance to India. As the sailors rowed toward its shore, Marco watched men fishing for pearls. They tied ropes around their bodies and dove to the bottom of the sea to gather the oysters. They stayed underwater for what seemed like an impossibly long time. Marco's junk passed them and landed in a port crowded with merchant ships from many countries.

The largest and most beautiful pearls were saved for the local ruler, who paid handsomely for them. He wore strings of pearls around his neck, as well as a collar made of sapphires, emeralds, and rubies. He had bracelets on his arms and rings on his toes and fingers, yet he wore only a simple loincloth to cover his body.

At the time of Marco's visit, southern India was broken into several independent empires. A Muslim dynasty controlled the north. Muslim warriors had fought their way over the northern mountains, then set themselves up as rulers.

✖ ✖ ✖

From times beyond written history, invaders were spurred on by stories of India's wealthy cities and golden temples. As far back as 3000 B.C., people grew wheat, barley, and cotton in the rich soil along the Indus River. They built two great cities there—Mohenjodaro and Harappa—and protected them behind thick stone walls. The people of these cities lived in brick houses and enjoyed some of the world's very first bathrooms! They sent ships loaded with their cotton, copper, and gold to cities far to the west.

This great civilization grew and thrived, then suddenly declined. The cities were abandoned and the region was invaded by people called Aryans, who left central Asia to sweep into Europe, Persia, and the Indus River valley.

Alexander the Great and his troops were among the many invaders who crossed the Indus River to overrun India. They clashed with Indian soldiers who charged them from the backs of elephants. Though Alexander's army was victorious, his men were weary of war (they had fought all the way from Greece to India) and wanted to go home. Alexander turned back.

Around 300 B.C, India's first emperor, Chandragupta, came to power. He conquered many of the separate regions of India and built one great empire, the Maurya Dynasty. His grandson, Asoka, went to war against the remaining regions until nearly all of India, from the towering mountains of the north to the great plains of the south, was under Maurya

Adam's Peak

The mountaintop shrine where the Buddha's relics were kept is still a sacred place in Sri Lanka. At the top of a mountain called Adam's Peak is a giant footprint created long ago. Buddhists believe it is the footprint of Buddha. Hindus believe it was left by one of their greatest gods, Siva. Muslims believe it was left by Adam after he was banned from the Garden of Eden.

Asoka's Pillar

control. Nothing could stop this bloodthirsty conqueror. But one day after a battle, he stopped and looked at the thousands of bodies strewn across the battlefield. He became horrified by his actions and the bloodshed he had caused. Emperor Asoka turned away from violence. He had the teachings of Buddha carved on stone pillars and placed all over the country. He encouraged his people to follow the way of peace, to be kind to each other and to all animals.

The following centuries were times of turmoil and invasion. The fourth century saw the rise of the Gupta Dynasty, one of the great civilizations of the world. Emperor Samudragupta expanded the borders of his realm by sending a white horse out to roam freely over the land. All of the land that the horse crossed in one year, he proclaimed, would become part of his empire. Splendid art and literature were created during the era of the Gupta Dynasty. Indian scholars made breakthroughs in mathematics and astronomy. They invented the system of numbers (mistakenly called Arabic numerals) that we use today, and they even came up with the concept of zero. In an age when some Europeans still thought they could sail off the edge of a flat earth, Indian scholars had calculated that the world was round.

A series of invasions caused the downfall of the Guptas. The White Huns, horsemen from

Asia, tumbled over the mountain passes and burned Indian villages and cities. They entered as conquerors but quickly became absorbed into Indian society. Then, in the seventh century, 16-year-old King Harsha took power. He raised an army of 50,000 men and 5,000 elephants and went to battle against a neighboring king who had kidnapped his sister.

When Harsha was done with war, he turned to matters of peace. He had temples built, and hospitals for the poor. Every five years he gave away all of his money and belongings. One year he gave until he had nothing left and had to borrow some clothes for himself!

Harsha died with no heirs, and his empire died with him. Dynasties rose and fell in the south of India. Then a new threat came from over the mountains in the north. Muslim warriors attacked the borders of India 17 times, until finally they overcame every last defense. The Muslims ruled India for five centuries.

✖ ✖ ✖

In India, Marco saw monks who slept on bare earth and ate very sparingly. They were Hindu yogis, who were practicing their religion as taught in their sacred scriptures, the Vedas. The Vedas described a system of hereditary social classes called the caste system. It gave strict rules on how people of different castes

Krishna

Say It in Hindi

Hindi is the official language of India (just one of many spoken there). Some words from India you already know—like *pajamas*, *bandanna*, and *calico* (a cloth first mentioned by Marco). Here are some more to add to your vocabulary:

Hello: Namaste (*na-mah-steh*)

Good-bye: Namaste (*na-mah-steh*)

Please: Mehrbaanii (*meh-her-bah-nee*)

Thank you: Sukria (*shoo-kree-a*)

Yes: Jii hã (*jee hahn*)

No: Jii Nah~i (*jee na-hee*)

The Vedas also described the many gods of Hinduism, all different faces of one universal spirit. Brahma (the Creator) is the four-faced god who is always creating new realities. Siva is the Destroyer. He dances constantly within the circle of the universe, making and unmaking worlds. Vishnu, the Preserver, appeared on earth nine times to protect the universe from danger. Once he came as a fish, and once as a lion. As the great hero Krishna, he did battle with demons and fell in love with the milkmaid Radha. As Prince Rama, he rescued his wife in deadly single combat with the 10-headed King Ravana.

In the Hindu religion, the soul reincarnates until it is purified and can return to its source. The actions a person takes in each life create consequences for the soul's future (this belief is known as *karma*). Good actions are rewarded; bad actions are punished, in either this lifetime or the next.

The strict Hindu monks and hermits that Marco saw were vegetarians because they believed that all living things have souls. As Marco told it, "They don't deprive any creature of life, not even a fly." They swept the ground before them so they wouldn't accidentally step on any insects. They held special reverence for the cow, a sacred animal.

Marco wrote that the Indian ruler he met had 1,000 wives and thousands of servants and

should behave, who they could marry, what they could eat, and how they should worship. Each of the four castes—priests, warriors, farmers, and servants—had its own sacred duty (dharma) to fulfill. Later, a fifth caste was added, that of the "untouchables." These were people who worked with the dead.

bodyguards to protect him. At that time, it was customary when a ruler died for all of his servants and wives to throw themselves into the fire in which his body was burned (a tradition called *suttee*). In this way, they could follow him to his next life.

According to another custom, if a person owed someone money, the creditor could demand his or her money back by drawing a circle around that person. The person could not move out of the circle, under punishment of death, until he or she paid the creditor. One day, Marco saw a merchant draw a circle around the king! The king stopped in his tracks and paid the merchant the money he owed him. Bystanders thought very highly of their ruler for not considering himself above the law.

Marco visited temples where young maidens danced and played musical instruments. Several times a day, they placed food at the feet of bronze statues of gods. Some of the statues portrayed gods dancing the universe into being. Other gods were shown seated with their legs crossed, in meditation. Some had four arms; others had the heads of elephants or lions.

Marco explored provinces up and down India's coasts, only touching the edges of the vast land. To the north, in a mountainous country rich with diamonds, he heard that people sent eagles swooping down into deep, hid-

Brahmin bull

den valleys to pick up the gems. To the south, people made beautiful violet-blue dye (indigo) from the roots of plants. The stifling heat of this country didn't stop merchants from many lands from coming to its ports to trade. They loaded their ships with dye and incense, with sacks of ginger and pepper, and with fine cloths embroidered with gold thread.

Pirate ships lay in wait out in the ocean, ready to prey on the fully loaded ships of the traders. The pirates ("of the most desperate character" wrote Marco) anchored their ships five miles apart and, when a merchant ship was

Indian tapestry

spotted, signaled to each other to close in for the attack. The pirates spent so much time at sea that they even had their wives and children on board with them!

The animals Marco saw in India were different from any he'd seen in his travels: black panthers, apes as large as people, huge white parrots, and strutting peacocks. After Marco saw the animals and the temples, the mountains and forests, the port cities, and the different customs of the people of India, he concluded that this was the "noblest country in the world."

ACTIVITY

Spiced Tea

"Not for all the tea in China," people say, even though today most of the world's tea comes from Sri Lanka and India. From the first cup served to an emperor of ancient China to the shipload dumped during the Boston Tea Party, tea has a long and illustrious history. Here's a recipe for tea that's great hot or iced.

What you need

2 cups water

Pot

2 bags orange pekoe and pekoe cut black tea

1/8 teaspoon ground ginger

1-inch stick of cinnamon

3 whole cloves

1/2 teaspoon ground cardamon

Dash of nutmeg

2 teaspoons sugar

1 tablespoon honey

Teapot

Fine-meshed strainer or coffee filter

1 cup milk

Boil the water in the pot. Place all the ingredients except the milk in the teapot. Allow it to steep for 5 minutes. Strain the tea into a cup through the fine-mesh strainer or coffee filter. Serve hot with warm milk or cold with milk and ice.

Wayang-kulit (Shadow-Puppet Play)

In the ancient tradition of Indonesian wayang-kulit *(shadow-puppet plays), a puppeteer (called a* dalang) *moves flat puppets from behind a backlit screen. The puppets act out stories of evil demons, bold heroes, and magic swords.*

What you need

Pencil

Cardboard (use the backs from pads of paper)

Scissors

Hole puncher

Paper fasteners

Tape

2 chopsticks

Rope

White sheet

Lamp

1 Using your pencil, draw your puppet on the cardboard, then cut it out. Make the head, body, and one of the arms all in one piece. Cut the other arm out in two pieces. (If you want your puppet to hold a sword, cut the sword so that it is one piece with the hand.) Punch a hole in the body at the place where the arm will be attached. Punch holes in both ends of the upper arm. Punch a hole where the elbow would be on the lower arm. Line the holes up, insert paper fasteners in each, and close them. Punch a hole for the eye.

2 Tape one of the chopsticks to the back of the puppet. Tape the other to the back of the hand. Practice moving the chopsticks to make the puppet move.

3 Make several puppets and invite friends to help you put on a show. Tie the rope across your room and drape the sheet over it. Place a bright lamp behind the sheet. Seat the audience in front. You and the other dalangs should narrate the story while ducking low and operating the puppets from behind the sheet. The puppet in this drawing is Prince Rama, who did battle with 10-headed King Ravana (see page 97). His story is one of the most popular shadow-plays performed.

Try Some Yoga

The Hindu practice of yoga, a discipline that leads to union of spirit and body, is more than 5,000 years old. There are actually six different kinds of yoga, but the one we are most familiar with is Hatha ("forceful") yoga. Gurus teach their disciples poses, called asanas, which require great fitness, determination, and control. These poses awaken the body's kundalini shakti (serpent power). They also exercise every muscle and part of the body. Here are three Hatha yoga poses: the Tree, the Lion, and the Cobra.

What you need

A quiet space with a flat surface

Exercise mat or rug

Comfortable clothes to wear

The Tree

Stand straight, looking forward, with your feet together and your arms at your sides. Slowly bend your right leg at the knee and raise your right foot. Place the sole of the foot as high as you possibly can on the inside of your left thigh. Balancing on your left foot, raise your arms over your head, keeping the elbows straight, and join your palms together above your head. Hold completely still and breathe gently in and out 10 times. Lower your arms and right leg. Stand still as you did at the beginning. Repeat with opposite leg.

The Lion

Sit on your knees with the heels of your feet against your buttocks. Place the balls of your hands on your knees, keeping your arms and back straight and looking straight ahead. Lean forward, open your mouth really wide, stick out your tongue as far as you can, cross your eyes, and stretch out your fingers. Hold this posture while you inhale, then exhale and relax. Repeat three to five times.

The Cobra

Lie on your stomach with your head turned to one side and arms along your sides, palms up. Turn your head and put your chin on the floor. Inhale. While you exhale, bring your arms up, place your hands on the floor beneath your shoulders with your forearms flat against the floor. Inhale. Press down on your hands and slowly lift yourself up from the waist, arching your spine and straightening your arms. Tilt your head far back and hold. Exhale and return to the original position.

6 The Tale Is Told

Marco returned once again to the court of Kublai Khan. It had been many years since he first appeared before the Khan's throne. He'd spent 3 years in one city and 14 years traveling to and from the many other provinces and kingdoms in and beyond the Khan's realm. Between journeys, he reported to Kublai Khan on the customs of the people, their trade, and their lands. Kublai Khan was always eager to hear Marco's stories and called him into his presence as soon as Marco

returned to the palace. The Khan's other advisers were very jealous of Marco.

Niccolo and Maffeo had accumulated great wealth during the years Marco served as the Khan's eyes and ears. Still, they were homesick and wanted to return to Venice. As the Khan grew older, they began to worry about what might happen to them when the ruler died. If the Chinese people revolted against their Mongol rulers, would the Polos be killed along with them? Also, the Khan's advisers, who had become jealous of Marco, might plot against him. The Polos could be in great danger.

But they couldn't leave without Kublai Khan's permission. One day, Niccolo threw himself at the feet of the ruler and explained that he and his son and brother had been away from home for 20 years—a very long time. "For our family's sake," he begged, "please let us go."

The Khan was hurt by the request. He did not want his foreign friends to leave his court, and he refused to give the Polos permission to leave. Instead, he offered to double the amount of their wealth. Time and again, they asked the Khan for permission to depart. "Nothing would persuade him to give us leave," Marco wrote.

One day, couriers arrived at the court of Kublai Khan. They carried a message from Arghun, the Mongol Khan of Persia. He had a special request for his overlord. His wife had died, and her last request had been that, when he remarried, it would be to a woman of her own Mongol tribe. Would the Great Khan choose a new bride for him from among the Mongol princesses?

Kublai Khan was happy to grant the request. Soon the young and beautiful Princess Kokachin was chosen to marry Arghun. With a large escort of armed guards, she was sent off on the journey to Persia. They rode for eight months over the roads Marco had traveled so long ago. One day, they realized they could go no farther. Terrible wars had broken out between rival tribes along the route, and it was far too dangerous to continue. The princess's escort brought her back to Kublai Khan's court.

Marco had just returned from his latest journey when Princess Kokachin and her escort reappeared. When the Khan began to worry about how to transport the young bride to her groom, Marco and his father and uncle approached him with a plan. They could take the young princess to Persia by sea, they suggested, avoiding the war that raged near the overland route. Marco knew at least part of the way by sea, and his father and uncle were expe-

Persian tile

rienced mariners. The Khan was sorry to lose his friends, but he agreed that the plan was a good one. The Polos turned their minds toward home and began planning for the long journey.

Kublai Khan spared no expense in outfitting them for the voyage. He ordered a fleet of 14 junks for his friends and had the junks filled with two years' worth of supplies. The Khan wrote letters to the Pope and to the kings of Europe and gave them to Marco to deliver. He gave the Polos gifts of rubies, sapphires, and other precious stones and said farewell to his long-time visitors.

The Elephant Bird

In the Arabian-Persian fables known as the Thousand and One Nights, Sindbad the Sailor saw a "bird of monstrous size called the roc, which fed its young on elephants." These stories and Marco's report of the huge bird of Madagascar were actually based on fact. A giant bird did once exist in Madagascar. The flightless elephant bird was eight feet tall, weighed 1,000 pounds, and laid two-gallon eggs—but it didn't eat elephants!

Marco wondered sadly if he would ever see Kublai Khan again, but as the fleet set out to sea, his spirits rose. There were still adventures ahead and at the end of them—home.

The junks stopped at many of the ports Marco had visited as the Khan's emissary. They sailed across the South China Sea and in three months came to port at the island of Sumatra. Bad weather delayed them there for months. When they were able to set sail again, they pointed their prows west. The junks hugged the coast of India, stopping at various ports for water and supplies.

The fleet seemed cursed with bad luck. They suffered mishaps at every turn. Shipwrecks, storms at sea, illness, and pirates took their toll. By the time they rounded India, only dozens of the hundreds of sailors and passengers who had begun the journey were still alive.

During the long months of their sea journey, the sailors told Marco stories of strange lands. Some of their stories were fanciful and some were based on facts. They told of a tribe of people living in the mountains of Sumatra who had long tails like monkeys. They spoke of the Island of Men and the Island of Women in the seas far to the south of India, where each sex lived on their own and only visited the other once a year. Farther south, they said, the people of a distant island collected ambergris, a sub-stance from the belly of whales, that washed up on their beaches. They sold it to traders on passing ships, who used it to make costly perfumes. Pirates were attracted by the wealth to be gained from the ambergris trade but, the sailors said, were terrified of the island's magicians. The magicians could make a calm sea rise into a terrible storm that no ship could survive.

Far to the west, off the coast of Africa, tigers and elephants roamed the forests of Madagascar. So did a large spotted animal with a very long neck—the giraffe (called a camelopard in ancient times by people who thought it looked like a cross between a spotted leopard and a camel). The people of Madagascar also claimed that once a year a giant bird, the Roc, flew over the island. They said it could seize an elephant in its talons and lift it into the air! Marco asked everyone about this marvelous bird but could get no proof of its existence. Could such a creature be?

In Zanzibar, north along the African coast, lived a warlike people, "brave in battle and contemptuous of death." They rode their camels and elephants into battle, throwing swords, lances, and stones at their enemies. Before going into combat, Marco said, they made their elephants drunk with wine so they would be "more furious in the assault."

Marco Polo lands at Ormuz

The sailors told Marco more stories of lands across the seas, but other adventurers would have to investigate them. The Polos were charged with getting Princess Kokachin safely to her destination. Finally, they reached the port of Ormuz and left their ships for the court of Arghun Khan.

When they brought the princess to the ruler's court, they found that Arghun Khan had died while they were making their way to his realm. His son Ghazan made them welcome, and they stayed with him for many months. There would be a marriage after all. According to Mongol tradition, the son would marry his father's intended bride.

The Polos witnessed the wedding of the princess to Ghazan. Then, with their obligation fulfilled, they began to prepare for the next stage of their journey. Ghazan Khan provided them with horses, camels, and supplies. Princess Kokachin cried when Marco said good-bye. They'd become close friends during their long journey.

Marco as a man

The Polos crossed Persia, heading to Trebizond, a city on the Black Sea. As they stopped in one village along the way, they heard news from the east—Kublai Khan had died. Marco mourned for the ruler who had been so kind to him, and he knew, now that the Khan was dead, that he would never see China again.

Just as they neared Trebizond, the Polos' caravan was attacked by bandits. The thieves made off with their horses and camels and stole their goods, including many of the treasures the Polos had brought from the east. Still, they had enough left to hire a ship in Trebizond to take them across the Black Sea. They sailed to Constantinople and from there to Venice. As they neared the coast, Marco scanned the horizon for the familiar domes and spires of the home he had left 24 years ago.

Marco and his father and uncle had changed greatly since they'd left on their long journey. Their clothes were ragged from travel. They looked like Mongols from the northern steppes. Marco, only a boy when they sailed away from Venice, was now 39 years old. Heads turned as they made their way through the streets of Venice toward their family home. Soon they stood at its gate.

The gatekeeper didn't believe their story. He didn't recognize them and was reluctant to let the Polos enter their own home. Their family had given up all thought of seeing them again, believing them long dead. Finally, the gate-keeper opened the doors and the Polos stood before their relatives. After long minutes, they were recognized as the lost travelers and given a hearty and happy welcome home.

A story is told of an unusual celebration the Polos held on their return. After they'd rested a few days, it is said, Marco and his father and uncle invited all of their friends and relatives to a banquet. No one refused. Everyone was curious to see these men who claimed to be Marco, Niccolo, and Maffeo.

A magnificent meal was served, one to rival those at the Khan's palace. The three Polos wore their costliest, most beautiful silk robes as they entertained their guests. Everyone admired the robes, each worth a family's fortune. They were very surprised when suddenly the Polos ripped off their fine robes and stood before them in their tattered traveling clothes. Then, to their greater surprise, the Polos ripped open the seams of these garments. Diamonds, emeralds, rubies, and sapphires spilled out of their clothes and onto the floor before them. They had sewn the gems inside their clothing as a safeguard against bandits.

In addition to the gems, Marco had returned to Venice with mementos of some of the places he had visited. He had gathered

Are We There Yet?

Marco traveled 20,000 miles on his 24-year-long journey.

seeds of plants from the islands and India and musk from the musk deer of China. He also brought home the wool of a yak, silks, and other rich fabrics embroidered with golden threads. He had the headdress of a Mongol woman and the armor of a Mongol warrior. A golden tablet from the Khan was one of his treasured possessions, and so were the beads he'd obtained from a Buddhist lama. A Mongol servant, Peter, had accompanied him back from his travels.

Marco settled into the life of a Venetian merchant, but he wasn't allowed to live quietly for very long. His city was at war with its rival—the Italian city of Genoa. Marco was asked to command a ship in a naval war between the two cities. His ship was captured in a violent sea battle and Marco was taken prisoner. Along with other captives, he was confined to a tower in Genoa, his fate uncertain.

The days were long in prison. Marco and his fellow prisoners spent hours speculating on their future and talking about their pasts.

Frontispiece for Marco Polo's book

When Marco told the story of his life, the others were stunned. Never had they heard such tales. His descriptions of Kublai Khan's palace, of the many countries of the vast Mongol empire, of the strange people and animals he had seen, were unlike anything they had ever heard.

One prisoner in particular was fascinated by Marco's stories. This man, Rustichello of Pisa, was a writer who knew a good story when he heard one. He asked Marco many questions and begged for details. One day, he asked Marco if he could help him write the story of his travels.

Marco was happy to have his story made into a book. He wrote to his father in Venice, asking him to send the notes he had taken over the years. He used his notes and his memory to tell the details of his 24-year journey to Rustichello, who diligently wrote down the story. By the time the two men were released after three years in prison, Marco's story was a book. They decided to call it *The Description of the World*.

Some people scoffed at the book and its title—*The Description of the World*? How could such a world be? The book described a world of heathens and barbarians, of animals with horns like unicorns and people who decorated their bodies with ink. Most absurd, people thought, were the descriptions of prosperous cities 10 times bigger than those of Europe and of a civilization more ancient and advanced than their own. Everyone knew that couldn't be true! They refused to believe that such a world existed and said that Marco's book contained millions of lies. They nicknamed him Marco of the Millions.

Others saw truth in Marco's story. Soon his book was translated into many languages. In those times books were copied by hand, and it seemed as if copyists couldn't work fast enough to make manuscripts in French and Latin, Spanish, German, and other languages. Everyone wanted to read about the caravan journey to the east and the marvels of the distant lands.

Marco married and with his wife, Donata, had three daughters. He settled down again in Venice and lived the rest of his life as a successful merchant. When he watched his ships arrive at Venice's wharves and saw the sailors unload goods from countries in the distant east, he thought of his adventures in those faraway lands. When the ships set off on their trading journeys, he felt a pull at his heart for the adventures that lay ahead of them.

Copies of Marco's book reached the courts of kings and the libraries of the powerful. It became more commonly known as *The Travels*. Geographers studied the manuscript and drew maps based on Marco's descriptions. Later adventurers confirmed the accuracy of Marco's reports of the countries to the east. (Sometimes it took a while—Marco's description of Japan was not confirmed until the 16th century.) The new geographical information Marco had provided was vast—he had opened a door to a new world.

This new world struck some as an opportunity to grow rich. Traders read the book and dreamed of new markets and great wealth. Others looked at *The Travels* as a marvelous tale about fantastic lands. Though Marco didn't describe any one-footed people or talking dragons, the tales he told were just as extraordinary. One person who read the book was inspired by its descriptions. He wrote notes in its margins and took it along with him on his own great journey. This person was Christopher Columbus, who tried to reach the lands Marco described by sailing to the west across the Atlantic.

Marco's book entertained many people, taught still others, and inspired a few to follow his footsteps. These explorations changed the world. He also changed the way Europeans thought about the world and about themselves. The world was bigger place than they had imagined, full of people and animals and marvels beyond anything they had ever seen. There were other religions, art, and customs. Theirs was not the only or even the oldest civilization.

A Book of Wonders

Marco's book is still in print, 700 years after he told his story to Rustichello. His *The Description of the World* begins:

"Lords, emperors and kings, dukes and marquesses, counts, knights and townsfolk and all people who wish to know of the various generations of men and the diversities of diverse regions of the world, take this book and have it read to you. Here you will find all the great marvels and the great diversities of the world. . . ."

The Ming and the Qing

The Ming emperors restored the Great Wall against further invasions. They built the Imperial City on the site of Kublai Khan's old palace. This residence still stands. It became known as the Forbidden City, because all men (except the emperor) were forbidden to be inside it at night. During the Ming Dynasty, Chinese sailors undertook seven long sea voyages to explore new lands. After this, China closed itself off from the rest of the world for many years.

In 1644, another great rebellion took place and, while the country was in turmoil, invaders from the north (the Manchus) took over. They established a new dynasty, the Qing, and ordered all their subjects to wear their hair in the Manchu-style pigtail. The Qing Dynasty ruled for three centuries, until 1911, when the last Chinese emperor, a six-year-old boy, was dethroned.

Soon after the Polos returned from their journey, the land route they had followed was closed by Muslim and Turkish armies. By the time other seafaring explorers reached the east, many things had changed.

After Kublai Khan died, his body was carried to a distant mountain range and buried according to Mongol tradition. His grandson, Temur, took his throne. He would be the last of the Mongol emperors of China. Temur was wicked and corrupt. More than ever, the people of China were unhappy under Mongol rule. Years of famine and great floods left many people hungry and homeless, but they received no help from Temur Khan. As things grew worse, the Chinese people began to plan an uprising.

The leaders of the rebellion had to be very careful so they wouldn't be caught plotting against the new Khan. The Mongols placed spies everywhere. The rebels met secretly in small groups. They hid messages for each other inside the special cakes that the Chinese people made to celebrate the full moon. When their plans were set, they put messages inside the little cakes telling everyone to rise up in mutiny against their Mongol overlords on the night of the next full moon.

On that night, the Chinese rebels invaded the palace and drove away their overlords. Temur Khan, with his empresses and concubines, fled

A Marco Polo Scrapbook

Rustichello wrote Marco's story in words, but there's more than one way to tell a tale. Playwrights and actors dramatize stories; photojournalists tell them with photographs. A scrapbook is a fun way to tell a story. Make a scrapbook of Marco's adventures! Use art—painting, calligraphy, collage, poetry—to tell the story.

What you need

Sketchbook or journal

Paints

Paint brushes

Markers

Scissors

Old magazines for clippings

Old postcards and notecards

Old maps

Glue

Miscellaneous items such as foil, yarn, feathers, colorful cloth

1 Go back through this book and think about the different parts of Marco Polo's journey. Break it down into sections. You'll devote one page in your scrapbook to each section. You could divide Marco's journey geographically—starting in Venice, the city of canals, and traveling through ancient Persia with its mosaics and bazaars, the lands of the Mongols, where people lived in round *gers* and rode horses across the steppes, to China, where powerful emperors built Great Walls and the Khan ruled from a magnificent palace. From there, you'll move to lush and exotic Indonesia, and India, with its elephants and temples. Or you could divide the story by traditions and customs—devote a page to each region's religions, ceremonies, and traditional dress. Perhaps you can think of other ways to present Marco Polo's journey.

2 For each page of your scrapbook, use art to interpret the geography or customs of the land. Use paints, markers, clippings from magazines, or any other objects to create a collage that represents that country or custom. For Persia, for instance, you might want to make a collage that looks like a mosaic, a traditional art form of ancient Persia. You can cut small pieces of different colored paper and glue them in the scrapbook, leaving a little white space between them, in the shapes of camels, palaces, an oasis in a desert. You can use Chinese brush strokes on your China page to paint wise mandarins, beautiful ladies in silk robes, dragons, and tigers. Look for pictures in the old magazines and cards that represent Indonesia—green jungles, spices, bright birds. Perhaps you'd like to devote pages to the religions of the east. Paste gold foil in your scrapbook in the shape of a temple and draw four-armed Siva dancing within a circle of fire. Use colorful cloths to make Tibetan prayer flags. Make a Silk Road page, or one with the animals of China (pandas, musk deer) or India (elephants, peacocks). You can write poems or short stories in the scrapbook, too. Title each page with creative lettering.

3 You can make a scrapbook like this of your own adventures. It's a great way to preserve memories of vacations and friends.

to the Mongol stronghold of Karakorum. He found no refuge there. The Buddhist lama who was the leader of the rebellion marched his troops to the Mongol capital and destroyed it. He became the first emperor of the next dynasty of China, the Ming. This dynasty reigned for nearly 300 years.

The fame and controversy about his book lasted all of Marco's life. Some people believed him, while others were sure that his book was nothing but a pack of lies. Even on his deathbed, some of his friends begged him to take back his story so he wouldn't die with a lie on his conscience. When the priest came to hear his final confession, he too warned Marco not to go to his death with lies unconfessed. Marco stood by his story. He told the priest, "I have not told the half of what I saw."

Glossary

Abacus: A tool with counters that are pushed along rods, used for performing calculations

Acupuncture: A Chinese medical treatment in which slender needles are inserted at specific points on the body in order to treat disease or pain

Aryan: An ancient nomadic people from Central Asia whose language is the root of many languages spoken today (including English, Italian, Hindi, and Persian)

Bazaar: A marketplace

Caliph: A Muslim ruler and spiritual leader

Calligraphy: The art of writing in elegant script

Caravan: An armed group of traders and merchants, with their animals and goods, who traveled together for protection against bandits

Cathay: The name Marco used for China

Concubine: A secondary wife

Crusades: The 11th–13th century military expeditions of European Christians to the eastern Mediterranean Christian holy lands

Dynasty: A series of rulers all descended from the same family

Emissary: A person sent on a mission as an agent of a government

Friar: A male member of a religious order

Griffin: A Greek mythological creature described as having the head and wings of an eagle and the body of a lion

Hangzhou: Marco called this great Chinese city Quinsai; located in a bay of the East China Sea, it was the imperial capital during the Song Dynasty

Horde: A clan or tribe, especially of Mongolian nomads

Java: This tropical island of Indonesia is about the size of England

Karakorum: The Mongolian capital built by Genghis Khan's son Ogodei, now a ruin in central Mongolia

Kashgar: Located in western China, this ancient trading center along the Silk Road is still known for its bazaar

Khan: A ruler, chief

Kowtow: To kneel and touch the forehead to the ground as an act of respect to a superior

Mandarin: A civil official of the ancient Chinese empires

Mecca: A city in Saudi Arabia which was the birthplace of Muhammad; Muslims make pilgrimages to this holy site

Nomad/Nomadic: unsettled, wandering people

Oasis: A place in a desert where water can be found

Ormuz (or Hormuz): The trade center Marco visited at the end of the Persian Gulf

Pagoda: A sacred tower or temple

Persepolis: An ancient capital of Persia, now in ruins

Post House: A house where horses were kept to hire out to travelers

Prophet: One who delivers divine messages

Quinsai: *See* Hangzhou

Roman Empire/Eastern Roman Empire:
The center of power in the western world beginning in 27 B.C.; the Roman Empire stretched across Europe, the Middle East, and North Africa, then it was divided into the Eastern Roman Empire and the Western Roman Empire in A.D. 395; the Eastern Roman Empire (called Byzantium) gained in power as the Western Empire fell before Germanic invaders; Emperor Constantine established the Byzantine capital in Constantinople (today's Istanbul); the Eastern (Byzantine) Roman Empire fell in 1453 to invading Turks

Satrap: A governor of a province in ancient Persia

Shang-tu: The Khan's summer residence, now To-lun in inner Mongolia; the winter residence, near today's Beijing, was Ta-tu (Marco called it Khanbaliq—"Khan's Town")

Steppe: A vast, treeless plain

Sultan: A Muslim ruler

Sumatra: A large, volcanic Indonesian island located on the equator

Tabriz: A 6,000-year-old trading center in northwest Iran (called Tauris in ancient times)

Takla Makan: A desert in the northwestern part of China, 600 miles long and 250 miles wide

Yam: The courier system of the Mongol Empire

Yin and Yang: In Chinese philosophy, yin stands for the female element, darkness, cold, and death; Yang stands for the male, light, heat, and life

Zhangye: An outpost along the Silk Road in the north part of China where the Polos stayed for many months

Biographies

Alexander the Great, 356–323 B.C., was one of the greatest generals in history. At only 20 years old, this young king of Macedonia (an ancient Greek kingdom) set out with his army to conquer the Greek city-states, the great Persian Empire, and lands from Egypt to India. He established cities from Alexandria in Egypt to Alexandria Eschate (meaning "farthest") in today's Afghanistan. There, he married the satrap's daughter, Roxana. His famous cavalry won victories against the armies of Persian King Darius and the war elephants of India. Alexander himself always rode his favorite horse, Bucephalus. After fighting his way to India, Alexander turned back. In Persia, he married the eldest daughter of the defeated king, Darius III, and began planning his next campaign. He died there at only 33 years old.

Batu, possibly 1203–1257, was the grandson of Genghis Khan. After Genghis Khan's death, the Mongol Empire was divided; Batu received com-mand of the western portion. With his army, the Golden Horde, he pushed the boundaries of his domain into eastern Europe, destroying whole cities and populations. Europe was saved from further destruction when Batu turned back to his homeland when his uncle Ogodei died.

Christopher Columbus, 1446–1506, was influ-enced by Marco Polo's travels to go on his own journeys of exploration. In 1492, the Italian mariner crossed the Atlantic Ocean hoping to discover a new route to the Far East. Instead, he discovered a land unknown to Europeans, America. A library in Spain holds Columbus's copy of *The Description of the World*, which has notes written in the margin by Columbus.

Constantine (Constantine the Great), 272–337, was born when the Roman Empire stretched across most of Europe, the Middle East, and northern Africa. The Roman Emperor appointed Constantine ruler of Britain and Gaul (France), but one day Constantine took an army against

Rome, conquered the imperial troops, and seized the Emperor's throne. He is remembered for two things—he made Christian worship lawful, and he moved the capital of the Roman Empire east, to the site of an ancient Greek city, Byzantium. Here, Constantine built a great new city and named it Constantinople (now known as Istanbul). The old Roman Empire fell into decline, and the new one, called the Byzantine Empire, prospered a thousand years.

Cyrus (the Elder or the Great) lived from approximately 580–529 B.C. He conquered many lands to found the empire of Persia and ruled it for 20 years. "I am Cyrus, the king of the world," he wrote on a clay cylinder. He was a merciful ruler who allowed his subjects to follow their own customs and religions.

Darius I (approximately 558–486 B.C.) was king of the Persian Empire several generations after Cyrus the Great. He conquered new lands, built the great city of Persepolis, and created an effective and powerful government. A later ruler, Darius III, lost this great empire to Alexander the Great.

Hulegu, 1217–1265, brother to Kublai Khan, defeated the Old Man of the Mountains and his Assassins, then moved against the Caliph of Baghdad. His terrible armies sacked the city and killed almost all of its people. They cut a path of destruction across Persia. Hulegu stayed to rule as Il-Khan of Persia until his death.

Ogodei, 1186–1241, son of Genghis Khan and Borte, became the Great Khan after his father's death. He finished the job his father started, sending his armies east against China, south against Tibet, and west toward Russia to conquer kingdoms and empires. He established regulations, laws, and systems to tax his subjects and built Karakorum as the Mongol capital.

Tamerlane (or Timur), 1336–1405, was born near Samarkand, the son of a Turkic-Mongol chieftain. He was wounded early in life and walked with a limp (the name we know him by comes from "Timur the Lame"). Ambition led him to falsely claim descent from Genghis Khan. He also borrowed a few tactics from the Mongol conqueror. Tamerlane subdued countries from India to the Mediterranean with an army of ruthless warriors. He showed no mercy (an early biographer said that Tamerlane "tore men to pieces like lions and overturned mountains"). During rare, peaceful moments, he played chess (he even invented a new version of it) and had history books read to him. As an old man, too weak to walk, he had himself carried at the head of his army on an invasion against China. He died on the way.

Web Sites to Explore

Explore these and other sites to learn about topics related to Marco Polo's journey.

China Vista

www.chinavista.com/discover.html
Take a virtual tour of the Forbidden City and a virtual walk along the Great Wall, as well as visiting other exciting places in China.

Chinese Astrology

www.cat.nyu.edu/liaos/horoscope.html
Are you a Rat or a Rooster? Learn more about your sign's qualities and read this year's forecast.

Daily Life in Ancient India

members.aol.com/Donnclass/Indialife.html
You'll feel like you were there after visiting this excellent site.

Empires Past

library.thinkquest.org/16325/indexie.shtml
Study at the library of ancient civilizations, then play an interactive game that takes you through ancient cities and introduces you to foreign cultures.

Foreign Languages

www.travlang.com/languages
Select any of 70 languages to learn basic words. Audio clips teach you how the words are supposed to sound.

The Inner Mongolia Museum

www.ezlink.com/~culturev/museum.html
Click on "Mongol herders" to visit a *ger*, and learn how the Mongol people lived.

The Metropolitan Museum of Art

www.metmuseum.org
Find amazing art and artifacts inside the Collections of the Met, from Ancient Near Eastern art, Asian art, Islamic art, and more.

National Geographic

www.nationalgeographic.com
Here you can find other countries, cultures, and worlds, as well as maps and articles about animals. Visit their special kids' site, too.

On-Line Chinese

www.mandarintools.com
Click on "Get a Chinese Name" to convert your English name to Chinese.

Tiger Information Center

www.5tigers.org
Here you can learn about tiger biology, behavior, and habitat as well as what you can do to help tigers in trouble.

World Wildlife Fund

www.worldwildlife.org
This site has a special page devoted to tigers where you can learn how these magnificent animals live, hunt, and mate. In the kid's section you'll find cool animal quizzes and games, including a "make a paper tiger" project.

The World Wildlife Fund's Just for Kids Site

www.panda.org/kids/kids.htm
Visit the "Animal Pages" to find out everything you ever wanted to know about elephants, tigers, rhinos, and more.

Bibliography

Anker, Charlotte, Russell B. Adams, Jr., and Charles J. Hagner, eds. *Persians: Masters of Empire*. Alexandria, VA: Time-Life Books, 1995.

Clayre, Alasdair. *The Heart of the Dragon*. Boston: Houghton Mifflin Company, 1985.

Einaudi, Giulio, ed. *The Travels of Marco Polo*. New York: The Orion Press, 1958.

Gernet, Jacques. *Daily Life in China on the Eve of the Mongol Invasion, 1250–1276*. Stanford, CA: Stanford University Press, 1962.

Glubok, Shirley. *The Art of China*. New York: The Macmillan Company, 1973.*

Larner, John. *Marco Polo and the Discovery of the World*. New Haven and London: Yale University Press, 1999.

Mackey, Sandra. *The Iranians: Persia, Islam and the Soul of a Nation*. New York: Dutton Signet, 1996.

Rossabi, Morris. *Khubilai Khan: His Life and Times*. Berkeley, Los Angeles, and London: University of California Press, 1988.

Sarwar, Ghulam. *Islam: Beliefs and Teachings*. London: The Muslim Educational Trust, 1989.

Schulberg, Lucille. *Historic India*. New York: Time-Life Books, 1968.

Severin, Tim. *Tracking Marco Polo*. New York: Peter Bedrick Books, 1964.

Smith, Huston. *The World's Religions*. New York: HarperCollins Publishers, 1991.

Suskind, Richard. *Cross and Crescent: The Story of the Crusades*. New York: W.W. Norton & Company, 1967.*

Tomasevic, Nebojsa, ed. *Tibet*. New York: McGraw-Hill, 1981.

*These books are recommended for young readers.

Photo Credits

Title page: The Great Wall of China. Courtesy of Northwest Archives.

Page xiv: The Polos leaving Venice. Courtesy of Northwest Archives.

Page 5: Caravan on the great highway of Central Asia. Courtesy of Northwest Archives.

Page 10: Genghis Khan on horseback. Courtesy of Northwest Archives.

Page 12: Colossal Persian bull's head. Courtesy of the Oriental Institute of the University of Chicago.

Page 13: Ruins of Persepolis. Courtesy of the Oriental Institute of the University of Chicago.

Page 16: *Old Man and Youth in Landscape*, Persian miniature from the early 16th century. Courtesy of the Freer Gallery of Art, Smithsonian Institution, Washington, DC, F1944.48a.

Page 24: The Great Wall of China. Courtesy of Northwest Archives.

Page 31: Maravijaya Buddha, Thailand (B60 S150+). Courtesy of The Asian Art Museum of San Francisco, The Avery Brundage Collection.

Page 32: The Great Wall of China. Courtesy of Northwest Archives.

Page 39: Nomadic Mongols moving camp. Courtesy of Northwest Archives.

Page 42: Marco Polo welcomed at the court of Kublai Khan. Courtesy of Northwest Archives.

Page 45: Tribute bearers, Handscroll (B60 D100 det). Courtesy of The Asian Art Museum of San Francisco, The Avery Brundage Collection.

Page 46: *The Three Teachings*, San-chiao t'u, Ming Dynasty (1368–1644). Hanging scroll, ink and color on silk. Courtesy of The Nelson-Atkins Museum of Art, Kansas City, MO (Gift of Bronson Trevor in honor of his father, John B. Trevor).

Page 49: A T'ang Palace. Courtesy of The Metropolitan Museum of Art, Rogers Fund, 1912 (12.37.133).

Page 64: *Chinese landscape*, Hanging scroll (B65 D53). Courtesy of The Asian Art Museum of San Francisco, The Avery Brundage Collection.

Page 67: Simhavaktra Dakini, Sino-Tibetan (B60 S600). Courtesy of The Asian Art Museum of San Francisco, The Avery Brundage Collection.

Page 68: Tibetan message boards, Tibet (1990.209). Courtesy of The Asian Art Museum of San Francisco, The Avery Brundage Collection.

Page 75: *Street Scenes in Times of Peace*, Zhu Yu (Junbi), Chinese, 1293–1365. Handscroll, ink and colors on paper, Yuan dynasty, mid-14th century, 26 x 790 cm, Kate S. Buckingham Fund, 1952.8

detail: *Merchants*. Photograph courtesy of The Art Institute of Chicago.

Page 77: *Cypress Tree*, Courtesy of Olivia Lenny Hill.

Page 88: The ships of Marco Polo. Courtesy of Northwest Archives.

Page 96: Kaliya Krishna (B65 B72). Courtesy of The Asian Art Museum of San Francisco, The Avery Brundage Collection.

Page 108: Marco Polo lands at Ormuz. Courtesy of Northwest Archives.

Page 109: Marco Polo, from a Venetian mosaic. Courtesy of Northwest Archives.

Page 111: Frontispiece from Polo's *Voyages*, published in Nuremberg, 1477. Courtesy of Northwest Archives.

Index

Other children's activity books by Janis Herbert

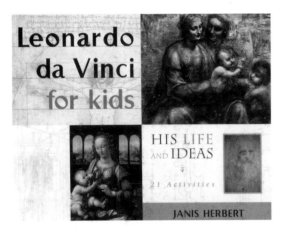

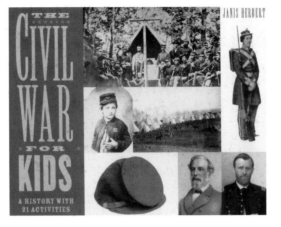

Leonardo da Vinci for Kids: His Life and Ideas, 21 Activities

"A lively biography of the ultimate Renaissance man. Herbert describes Leonardo's life while also providing a good deal of historical information about art." —*School Library Journal*

"Thoroughly illustrated and well designed, this is a fine purchase that rises above the current bounty of available books on the subject." —*Booklist*

The Civil War for Kids: A History with 21 Activities

"For children who *really* want to know what it felt like to take an active role in the past, *The Civil War for Kids* is *it*!" —*Civil War Book Review*

"Teachers and parents will find this book a very handy tool to help teach their students and children about this critical period in our nation's history." —D. Scott Hartwig, Historian, Gettysburg, Pennsylvania

Lewis and Clark for Kids: Their Journey of Discovery with 21 Activities

"The Lewis and Clark expedition was not only one of America's greatest adventures, it was one of our nation's greatest leaps in learning. Geography, ethnology, zoology, botany, and literature—the Corps of Discovery made important contributions to them all. This book invites readers to join Lewis and Clark's epic journey and helps them make their own discoveries along the way." —Dayton Duncan, author of *Out West: American Journey Along the Lewis and Clark Trail*